The Lady's not for Burning

CHRISTOPHER FRY

T H E

Lady's not for Burning

A C O M E D Y

1950
Oxford University Press
NEW YORK & LONDON

To ALEC CLUNES

CHARACTERS

(in order of their appearance)

RICHARD, *an orphaned clerk*
THOMAS MENDIP, *a discharged soldier*
ALIZON ELIOT
NICHOLAS DEVIZE
MARGARET DEVIZE, *mother of Nicholas*
HUMPHREY DEVIZE, *brother of Nicholas*
HEBBLE TYSON, *the Mayor*
JENNET JOURDEMAYNE
THE CHAPLAIN
EDWARD TAPPERCOOM, *a Justice*
MATTHEW SKIPPS

SCENE: *A room in the house of* HEBBLE TYSON, *Mayor of the small market-town of Cool Clary.*

TIME: 1400 *either more or less or exactly.*

The Lady's not for Burning

'In the past I wanted to be hung. It was worth while being hung to be a hero, seeing that life was not really worth living.'

A convict who confessed falsely to a murder, February 1947

Act One

The Scene (*the house of* HEBBLE TYSON, *the Mayor of the little market town of Cool Clary*) *and the appearance of the characters are as much fifteenth century as anything.*

RICHARD, *a young copying-clerk, stands working at a desk.* THOMAS MENDIP, *less young, in his late twenties perhaps, and less respectable, looks in through a great window from the garden.*

THOMAS. Soul!

RICHARD.   —and the plasterer, that's fifteen groats——

THOMAS. Hey, soul!

RICHARD.   —for stopping the draught in the privy——

THOMAS.   Body!
  You calculating piece of clay!

RICHARD.   Damnation.

THOMAS. Don't mention it. I've never seen a world
  So festering with damnation. I have left
  Rings of beer on every alehouse table
  From the salt sea-coast across half a dozen counties,
  But each time I thought I was on the way
  To a faintly festive hiccup
  The sight of the damned world sobered me up again.
  Where is the Mayor? I've business with His Worship.

RICHARD. Where have you come from?

THOMAS.   Straight from your local.
  Damnation's pretty active there this afternoon,
  Licking her lips over gossip of murder and witchcraft;
  There's mischief brewing for someone. Where's the Mayor?

RICHARD. I'm the mayor's clerk.

[3]

THOMAS.   How are you?
RICHARD. Can I have your name?
THOMAS.   It's yours.
RICHARD.   Now, look——
THOMAS.   It's no earthly
    Use to me. I travel light; as light,
    That is, as a man can travel who will
    Still carry his body around because
    Of its sentimental value. Flesh
    Weighs like a thousand years, and every morning
    Wakes heavier for an intake of uproariously
    Comical dreams which smell of henbane.
    Guts, humours, ventricles, nerves, fibres
    And fat—the arterial labyrinth, body's hell.
    Still, it was the first thing my mother gave me,
    God rest her soul. What were you saying?
RICHARD.   Name
    And business.
THOMAS.   Thomas Mendip. My well-born father,
    If birth can ever be said to be well, maintains
    A castle as draughty as a tree. At every sunset,
    It falls into the river and fish swim through its walls.
    They swim into the bosom of my grandmother
    Who sits late, watching for the constellation of Orion
    Because my dead grandfather, she believes,
    Is situated somewhere in the Belt.
    That is part of the glory of my childhood.
RICHARD. I like you as much as I've liked anybody.
    Perhaps you're a little drunk. But here, I'm afraid,
    They may not take to you.
THOMAS.   That's what I hope.
RICHARD. Who told you to come here?
    You couldn't have chosen a less fortunate afternoon.

[4]

They're expecting company—well, a girl. Excuse me,
I must get back to the books.

THOMAS.   I'll wait.

RICHARD.   He'll not
See anybody; I'm sure of it.

THOMAS.   Dear boy,
I only want to be hanged. What possible
Objection can he have to that?

RICHARD.   Why, no, I—
To be—*want* to be hanged? How very drunk you are
After all. Who ever would want to be hanged?

THOMAS.   You don't
Make any allowance for individuality.
How do you know that out there, in the day or night
According to latitude, the entire world
Isn't wanting to be hanged? Now you, for instance,
Still damp from your cocoon, you're desperate
To fly into any noose of the sun that should dangle
Down from the sky. Life, forbye, is the way
We fatten for the Michaelmas of our own particular
Gallows. What a wonderful thing is metaphor.

RICHARD. Was that a knock?

THOMAS.   The girl. She knocks. I saw her
Walking through the garden beside a substantial nun.
Whsst! Revelation!

Enter ALIZON ELIOT, *aged seventeen, talking to herself.*

ALIZON. Two steps down, she said. One, two,
The floor. Now I begin to be altogether
Different—I suppose.

RICHARD.   O God, God,
God, God, God. I can see such trouble!

[5]

Is life sending a flame to nest in my flax?
For pity's sake!

THOMAS.   Sweet pretty noose, nice noose.

RICHARD. Will you step in?

ALIZON.   They told me no one was here.

RICHARD. It would be me they meant.

ALIZON.   Oh, would it be?
Coming in from the light, I am all out at the eyes.
Such white doves were paddling in the sunshine
And the trees were as bright as a shower of broken glass.
Out there, in the sparkling air, the sun and the rain
Clash together like the cymbals clashing
When David did his dance. I've an April blindness.
You're hidden in a cloud of crimson Catherine-wheels.

RICHARD. It doesn't really matter. Sit in the shadow.

THOMAS. There are plenty to choose from.

ALIZON.   Oh, there are three of us!
Forgive me.

RICHARD.   He's waiting—he wants—he says——

THOMAS.   I breathe,
I spit, I am. But take no further notice.
I'll just nod in at the window like a rose;
I'm a black and frosted rosebud whom the good God
Has preserved since last October. Take no notice.

ALIZON. Men, to me, are a world to themselves.

RICHARD.   Do you think so?

ALIZON. I am going to be married to one of them, almost at
    once.
I have met him already.

RICHARD.   Humphrey.

ALIZON.   Are you his brother?

RICHARD. No. All I can claim as my flesh and blood
Is what I stand up in. I wasn't born,

[6]

I was come-across. In the dusk of one Septuagesima
A priest found an infant, about ten inches long,
Crammed into the poor-box. The money had all
Been taken. Nothing was there except myself,
I was the baby, as it turned out. The priest,
Thinking I might have eaten the money, held me
Upside down and shook me, which encouraged me
To live, I suppose, and I lived.

ALIZON.   No father or mother?

RICHARD. Not noticeably.

ALIZON.   You mustn't let it make you
Conceited. Pride is one of the deadly sins.

THOMAS. And it's better to go for the lively ones.

ALIZON.   Which ones
Do you mean?

THOMAS. Pay no heed. I was nodding in.

ALIZON. I am quite usual, with five elder sisters. My birth
Was a great surprise to my parents, I think. There had been
A misunderstanding and I appeared overnight
As mushrooms do. It gave my father thrombosis.
He thought he would never be able to find enough husbands
For six of us, and so he made up his mind
To simplify matters and let me marry God.
He gave me to a convent.

RICHARD. What showing did he think he would make as God's
Father-in-law?

ALIZON.   He let his beard grow longer.
But he found that husbands fell into my sisters' laps.
So then he stopped thinking of God as eligible—
No prospects, he thought. And so he looked round and found
me
Humphrey Devize. Do you think he will do?

[7]

RICHARD. Maybe.
He isn't God, of course.

ALIZON. No, he isn't.
He's very nearly black.

RICHARD. Swart.

ALIZON. Is that it?
When he dies it may be hard to picture him
Agreeable to the utter white of heaven.
Now you, you are——

RICHARD. Purgatory-colour.

ALIZON. It's on the way to grace. Who are you?

RICHARD. Richard,
The mayor's copying-clerk.

ALIZON. The mayor is Humphrey's
Uncle. Humphrey's mother is the mayor's sister.
And then, again, there's Nicholas, Humphrey's brother.
Is he sensible?

RICHARD. He knows his way about.

THOMAS. O enviable Nick.

RICHARD. He's nodding in.

ALIZON. I'll tell you a strange thing. Humphrey Devize
Came to the convent to see me, bringing a present
For his almost immediate wife, he said, which is me,
Of barley-sugar and a cross of seed-pearls. Next day
Nicholas came, with a little cold pie, to say
He had a message from Humphrey. And then he sat
And stared and said nothing until he got up to go.
I asked him for the message, but by then
It had gone out of his head. Quite gone, you see.
It was curious.—Now you're not speaking either.

RICHARD. Yes, of course; of course it was curious.

ALIZON. Men are strange. It's almost unexpected
To find they speak English. Do you think so too?

[8]

RICHARD. Things happen to them.

ALIZON. What things?

RICHARD. Machinations of nature;
As April does to the earth.

ALIZON. I wish it were true!
Show me daffodils happening to a man!

RICHARD. Very easily.

THOMAS. And thistles as well, and ladies'
Bedstraw and deadly nightshade and the need
For rhubarb.

ALIZON. Is it a riddle?

RICHARD. Very likely.
Certainly a considerable complication.

Enter NICHOLAS DEVIZE, *muddy, dishevelled.*

NICHOLAS. Where are you, Alizon? Alizon, what do you think?
The stars have blown all my way, by Providence!
It's me you're going to marry. What do you think
Of that?

RICHARD. You have mud in your mouth.

NICHOLAS. You canter off.

ALIZON. No, Nicholas. That's untrue. I have to be
The wife of Humphrey.

NICHOLAS. Heaven says no. Heaven
And all the acquiescent nodding of angels
Says Alizon for Nicholas, Nicholas for Alizon.
You must come to know me; not so much now, because
now
I'm excited, but I have at least three virtues.
How many have you got?

RICHARD. Are you mad? Why don't you
Go and clean yourself up?

[9]

NICHOLAS. What shall I do
With this nattering wheygoose, Alizon?
Shall I knock him down?

ALIZON. His name is Richard, he says;
And I think he might knock you down.

THOMAS. Nicholas,
He might. There you have a might, for once,
That's right. Forgive me; an unwarranted interruption.

NICHOLAS. Come in, come in.—Alizon, dear, this Richard
Is all very well. But I was conceived as a hammer
And born in a rising wind. I apologize
For boasting, but once you know my qualities
I can drop back into a quite brilliant
Humility. God have mercy upon me,
You have such little hands. I knew I should love you.

RICHARD. Just tell me: am I to knock him down? You have
only
To say so.

ALIZON. No, oh no. We only have
To be patient and unweave him. He is mixed,
Aren't you, Nicholas?

NICHOLAS. Compounded of all combustibles,
The world's inside. I'm the receipt God followed
In the creation. It took the roof off his oven.
How long will it be before you love me, Alizon?
Let's go.

[*He picks her up in his arms.*

Enter MARGARET DEVIZE.

MARGARET. Where are you taking Alizon, Nicholas?

NICHOLAS. Out into the air, mother.

MARGARET. Unnecessary.
She's in the air already. This room is full of it.

Put her down, Nicholas. You look
As though you had come straight out of a wheelbarrow;
And not even straight out. And the air so trim
And fresh. It is such a pity.

NICHOLAS.   I must tell you
I've just been reborn.

MARGARET.   Nicholas, you always think
You can do things better than your mother. You can be sure
You were born quite adequately on the first occasion.
There is someone here I don't know. Who is it, Alizon?
Did he come with you?

ALIZON.   Oh, no. A rosebud, he says.

MARGARET. A rosebud, Alizon?

ALIZON.   He budded in October.

MARGARET. He's not speaking the truth.—You're a pretty child
And mercifully without spots, unlike
The cowslip. O heavens, we have all been young,
Young all day long, young in and out of season,
In the dream, in the glass, in the firelight—
Perfectly young, obstreperously golden.
What a martyrdom it was.—Tch! more rain!
This is properly April.—And you're eager to see
Your handsome Humphrey. Nicholas will fetch him.
They're inseparable, really twin natures, utterly
Brothers, like the two ends of the same thought.—
Nicholas, dear, call Humphrey.

NICHOLAS.   I can't. I've killed him.

MARGARET. Fetch Humphrey, Nicholas dear.

NICHOLAS.   I've killed him, dearest
Mother.

MARGARET. Well, never mind. Call Humphrey, dear.

THOMAS. Is that the other end of this happy thought,
There, prone in the flower-bed?

[11]

RICHARD. Yes, it's Humphrey
Lying in the rain.

MARGARET. One day I shall burst my bud
Of calm, and blossom into hysteria.
Tell him to get up. Why on this patient earth
Is he lying in the rain?

THOMAS. All flesh is grass.

ALIZON. Have you really killed Humphrey?

MARGARET. Nicholas,
Your smile is no pleasure to me.

NICHOLAS. We fought for possession
Of Alizon Eliot. What could be more natural?
What he loves, I love. And if existence will
Molest a man with beauty, how can he help
Trying to impose on her the boundary
Of his two bare arms?—O pandemonium,
What a fight, what a fight! It couldn't be more strenuous
Getting into heaven, or out again. And Humphrey
Went twinkling like Lucifer into the daffodils.
When Babylon fell there wasn't a better thump.

MARGARET. Are you standing there letting your brother be
rained on?
Haven't you any love for him?

NICHOLAS. Yes, mother,
But wet as well as dry.

MARGARET. Can Richard carry him
Single-handed?

NICHOLAS. Why can't he use both hands?
And how did I know it was going to rain?

[*Exit* NICHOLAS *with* RICHARD.

MARGARET. I would rather have to plait the tails of unbroken
Ponies than try to understand Nicholas.

[12]

Oh! it's bell-ringing practice. Their ding-dong rocks me
Until I become the belfry, and makes bright blisters
All along my nerves. Dear God, a cuckoo
As well!

THOMAS.   By God, a cuckoo! Grief and God,
A canting cuckoo, that laugh with no smile!
A world unable to die sits on and on
In spring sunlight, hatching egg after egg,
Hoping against hope that out of one of them
Will come the reason for it all; and always
Out pops the arid chuckle and centuries
Of cuckoo-spit.

MARGARET.   I don't really think we need
To let that worry us now. I don't know why you're waiting,
Or who brought you, or whether I could even
Begin to like you, but I know it would be agreeable
If you left us. There's enough going on already.

THOMAS.   Bliss; indeed,
Extreme bliss. There is certainly
Enough going on. Madam, watch Hell come
As a gleam into the eye of the wholesome cat
When philip-sparrow flips his wing.
I see a gleam of Hell in *you*, madam.
You understand those bells perfectly.
I understand them, too.
What is it that, out there in the mellow street,
The soft rain is raining on?
Is it only on the little sour grass, madam?

MARGARET. Out in the street? What could it be?

THOMAS.   It could be,
And it is, a witch-hunt.

MARGARET.   Oh!—dear; another?

[13]

THOMAS. Your innocence is on at such a rakish angle
It gives you quite an air of iniquity.
By the most naked of compassionate angels
Hadn't you better answer that bell? With a mere
Clouding of your unoccupied eyes, madam,
Or a twitch of the neck: what better use can we put
Our faces to than to have them express kindness
While we're thinking of something else? Oh, be disturbed,
Be disturbed, madam, to the extent of a tut
And I will thank God for civilization.
This is my last throw, my last poor gamble
On the human heart.

MARGARET. If I knew who you were
I should ask you to sit down. But while you're on
Your feet, would you be kind enough to see
How Humphrey is doing?

THOMAS. If we listened, we could hear
How the hunters, having washed the dinner things,
Are now toiling up and down the blind alleys
Which they think are their immortal souls,
To scour themselves in the blood of a grandmother.
They, of course, will feel all the better for it.
But she? Grandma? Is it possible
She may be wishing she had died yesterday,
The wicked sobbing old body of a woman?

MARGARET. At the moment, as you know,
I'm trying hard to be patient with my sons.
You really mustn't expect me to be Christian
In two directions at once.

THOMAS. What, after all,
Is a halo? It's only one more thing to keep clean.
Richard and Nicholas
Have been trying to persuade the body to stand up.

[14]

ALIZON. Why, yes, he isn't dead. He's lying on his back
Picking the daffodils. And now they are trying
To lift him. I am sure that yellow and wet
Whistling is a blackbird. The hot sun
Is out again.

MARGARET.   Let me look over your shoulder.
They mustn't see me taking an interest.
Oh, the poor boy looks like a shock
Of bedraggled oats.—But you will see, Alizon,
What a nice boy he can be when he wears a clean shirt.
I more than once lost my heart to clean linen
When I was a young creature, even to linen
That hung on the hedges without a man inside it.
Do I seem composed, sufficiently placid and unmotherly?

ALIZON. Altogether, except that your ear-ring
Trembles a little.

MARGARET.   It's always our touches of vanity
That manage to betray us.

THOMAS.   When shall I see the mayor?
I've had enough of the horror beating in the belfry.
Where is the mayor?

Re-enter RICHARD *and* NICHOLAS, *carrying* HUMPHREY *who
has a bunch of daffodils in his hand.*

NICHOLAS.   Here's Humphrey. Where would you like him?

MARGARET. Humphrey, why do you have to be carried?

HUMPHREY.   My dear
Mother, I didn't knock myself down. Why
Should I pick myself up?—Daffodils
For my future wife.

NICHOLAS.   You slawsy poodle, you tike,
You crapulous puddering pipsqueak! Do I have to kill you
A second time? What about the stars?

[15]

HUMPHREY. All right;
What about the stars? They flicker and flicker, like hell's
Light they flicker.

NICHOLAS. You dismal coprolite!
Haven't they said that I shall have Alizon Eliot?

HUMPHREY. Astral delirium, dear Nick. Officially
Alizon is mine. What is official
Is incontestable. It undercuts
The problematical world and sells us life
At a discount.—Without disrespect either
To you, mother, or to my officially
Dear one, I shall lie down.—Who is playing the viol?

MARGARET. The Chaplain is tuning his G string by the bells.
It must be time for prayers. It must be time
For something. You're both transfigured with dirt.

THOMAS. Where in thunder is the mayor? Are you deaf to the
baying
Of those bib-and-tuckered bloodhounds out in the street?
I want to be hanged.

NICHOLAS [to HUMPHREY]. O blastoderm of injustice,
You multiplication of double-crossing! Wait
Till the dark comes and then go out if you dare
Bareheaded under the flash of my star Mercury.
Ignore the universe if you can. Go on,
Ignore it!—Alizon, who's going to marry you?

MARGARET. He deserves no answer.

RICHARD. Can you tell us, Alizon?

ALIZON. I am not very used to things happening rapidly.
The nuns, you see, were very quiet, especially
In the afternoon. They say I shall marry Humphrey.

MARGARET. Certainly so. Now, Nicholas, go and get clean.

NICHOLAS. She never shall!

[16]

THOMAS.   Will someone fetch the mayor?
Will no one make the least effort to let me
Out of the world?
NICHOLAS.   Let Humphrey go and officially
Bury himself. She's not for him.
What does love understand about hereinafter-
Called-the-mortgagee?
An April anarchy, she is, with a dragon's breath,
An angel on a tiger,
The jaws and maw of a kind of heaven, though hell
Sleeps there with one open eye; an onslaught
Unpredictable made by a benefactor
Armed to the teeth——
THOMAS.   Who benefits, before God,
By this concatenation of existences,
This paroxysm of the flesh? Let me get out!
I'll find the mayor myself wherever he may be having
His pomposity of snobjoy snores,
And you can go on with your psalm of love.
                              [*He makes for the door.*
HUMPHREY. Who the hell's that?
RICHARD.   The man about the gallows.

Enter HEBBLE TYSON, *the mayor, afflicted with office.*

MARGARET. Now here's your uncle. Do, for the sake of calm,
Go and sweeten yourselves.
THOMAS.   Is this the man
I long for?
TYSON.   Pest, who has stolen my handkerchief?
MARGARET. Use this one, Hebble.—Go and get under the
pump.
                              [*Exit* HUMPHREY *and* NICHOLAS.
TYSON [*blowing his nose*]. Noses, noses.

[17]

THOMAS.   Mr. Mayor, it's a joy to see you.
You're about to become my gateway to eternal
Rest.

TYSON. Dear sir, I haven't yet been notified
Of your existence. As far as I'm concerned
You don't exist. Therefore you are not entitled
To any rest at all, eternal or temporary,
And I would be obliged if you'd sit down.

MARGARET. Here is Alizon Eliot, Humphrey's bride
To be.

THOMAS. I have come to be hanged, do you hear?

TYSON. Have you filled in the necessary forms?—
So this is the young lady? Very nice, very charming.—
And a very pretty dress.
Splendid material, a florin a yard
If a groat. I'm only sorry you had to come
On a troubled evening such as this promises
To be. The bells, you know. Richard, my boy,
What is it this importunate fellow wants?

RICHARD. He says he wants to be hanged, sir.

TYSON.   Out of the question.
It's a most immodest suggestion, which I know
Of no precedent for. Cannot be entertained.
I suspect an element of mockery
Directed at the ordinary decencies
Of life.—Tiresome catarrh.—A sense of humour
Incompatible with good citizenship
And I wish you a good evening. Are we all
Assembled together for evening prayers?

THOMAS.   Oh no!
You can't postpone me. Since opening-time I've been
Propped up at the bar of heaven and earth, between
The wall-eye of the moon and the brandy-cask of the sun,

[18]

Growling thick songs about jolly good fellows
In a mumping pub where the ceiling drips humanity,
Until I've drunk myself sick, and now, by Christ,
I mean to sleep it off in a stupor of dust
Till the morning after the day of judgement.
So put me on the waiting-list for your gallows
With a note recommending preferential treatment.

TYSON. Go away; you're an unappetizing young man
With a tongue too big for your brains. I'm not at all sure
It would be amiss to suppose you to be a vagrant,
In which case an unfortunate experience
At the cart's tail——

THOMAS.   Unacceptable.
Hanging or nothing.

TYSON.   Get this man away from here!
Good gracious, do you imagine the gallows to be
A charitable institution? Very mad,
Wishes to draw attention to himself;
The brain a delicate mechanism; Almighty
God more precise than a clockmaker;
Grant us all a steady pendulum.
All say Amen.

THOMAS. Listen! The wild music of the spheres:
Tick-tock.

RICHARD.   Come on; you've got to go.

THOMAS. Does Justice with her sweet, impartial,
Devastating and deliberate sword
Never come to this place? Do you mean
There's no recognition given to murder here?

MARGARET. Murder?

TYSON.   Now what is it?

THOMAS.   I'm not a fool.
I didn't suppose you would do me a favour for nothing.

No crime, no hanging; I quite understand the rules.
But I've made that all right. I managed to do-in
A rag-and-bone merchant at the bottom of Leapfrog Lane.

TYSON [*staring*]. Utterly unhinged.

MARGARET.   Hebble, they're all
In the same April fit of exasperating nonsense.
Nicholas, too. He said he had killed Humphrey
But of course he hadn't. If he had I should have told you.

THOMAS. It was such a monotonous cry, that 'Raga-boa!'
Like the damned cuckoo. It was more than time
He should see something of another world.
But, poor old man, he wasn't anxious to go.
He picked on his rags and his bones as love
Picks upon hearts, he with an eye to profit
And love with an eye to pain.

RICHARD.   *Sanctus fumus!*

TYSON. Get a complete denial of everything
He has said. I don't want to be bothered with you.
You don't belong to this parish. I'm perfectly satisfied
He hasn't killed a man.

THOMAS.   I've killed two men
If you want me to be exact.
The other I thought scarcely worth mentioning:
A quite unprepossessing pimp with a birthmark.
He couldn't have had any affection for himself.
So I pulped him first and knocked him into the river
Where the water gives those girlish giggles around
The ford, and held him under with my foot
Until he was safely in Abram's bosom, birthmark
And all. You see, it still isn't properly dry.

TYSON. What a confounded thing! Who do people
Think they are, coming here without
Identity, and putting us to considerable

Trouble and expense to have them punished?
You don't deserve to be listened to.

THOMAS.   It's habit.
I've been unidentifiably
Floundering in Flanders for the past seven years,
Prising open ribs to let men go
On the indefinite leave which needs no pass.
And now all roads are uncommonly flat, and all hair
Stands on end.

Enter NICHOLAS.

NICHOLAS.   I'm sorry to interrupt
But there's a witch to see you, uncle.

TYSON.   To see me?
A witch to see me? I will not be the toy
Of irresponsible events. Is that clear
To you all?

NICHOLAS.   Yes. But she's here.

TYSON.   A witch to see me!
Do I have to tell you what to do with her?

NICHOLAS. Don't tell me. My eyes do that only too well.
She is the one, of witches she's the one
Who most of all disturbs Hell's heart. Jimminy!
How she must make Damnation sigh.
How she must make Torment be tormented
To have her to add to its torment! How the flames
Must burn to lay their tongues about her.
If evil has a soul it's here outside,
The dead-of-midnight flower, Satan's latest
Button-hole. Shall I ask her in?

THOMAS.   She's young,
O God, she's young.

[21]

TYSON.   I stare at you, Nicholas,
    With no word of condemnation. I stare,
    Astonished at your behaviour.
MARGARET.   Ask her in?
    In here? Nicholas——
THOMAS.   Nicholas! Expose
    The backside of immortality before ladies?
    Your mother would never be able to get the smell
    Of sulphur out of the curtains.
NICHOLAS.   She's the glorious
    Undercoat of this painted world——
                [JENNET JOURDEMAYNE *stands in the doorway.*
                                    ——You see:
    It comes through, however much of our whiteness
    We paint over it.
TYSON.   What is the meaning of this?
    What is the meaning of this?
THOMAS.   That's the most relevant
    Question in the world.
JENNET.   Will someone say
    Come in? And understand that I don't every day
    Break in on the quiet circle of a family
    At prayers? Not quite so unceremoniously,
    Or so shamefully near a flood of tears,
    Or looking as unruly as I surely do. Will you
    Forgive me?
TYSON.   You'll find I can't be disarmed
    With pretty talk, young woman. You have no business
    At all in this house.
JENNET.   Do you know how many walls
    There are between the garden of the Magpie,
    Past Lazer's field, Slink Alley and Poorsoul Pond
    To the gate of your paddock?

                        [22]

TYSON.   I'm not to be seduced.
I'm not attending.
JENNET.   Eight. I've come over them all.
MARGARET. How could she have done?
THOMAS.   Her broomstick's in the hall.
MARGARET. Come over to this side of the room, Nicholas.
NICHOLAS. Don't worry, mother, I have my fingers crossed.
TYSON. Never before in the whole term of my office
    Have I met such extraordinary ignorance
    Of what is permitted——
JENNET.   Indeed, I was ignorant.
    They were hooting and howling for me, as though echoes
    Could kill me. So I took to my toes. Thank God
    I only passed one small girl in a shady
    Ditch telling the beads of her daisy-chain.
    And a sad rumpled idiot-boy
    Who smiled at me. They say I have changed a man
    Into a dog.
TYSON.   This will all be gone into
    At the proper time——
JENNET.   But it isn't a dog at all.
    It's a bitch; an appealing, rueful, brindle bitch
    With many fleas. Are you a gentleman
    Full of ripe, friendly wisdom?
TYSON.   This
    Will all be gone into at the proper——
JENNET.   If so
    I will sit at your feet. I will sit anyway;
    I am tired. Eight walls are enough.
MARGARET.   What do we do?
    I can almost feel the rustling-in of some
    Kind of enchantment already.

[23]

TYSON.   She will have
   To be put in charge.
ALIZON.   Oh, must she, must she?
THOMAS. He can see she's a girl of property,
   And the property goes to the town if she's a witch;
   She couldn't have been more timely.
NICHOLAS.   Curious, crooked
   Beauty of the earth. Fascinating.
TYSON [to JENNET]. Get up at once, you undisciplined girl.
   Have you never
   Heard of law and order?
NICHOLAS.   Won't you use
   This chair?
JENNET.   Thank you. Oh, this is the reasonable
   World again! I promise not to leave behind me
   Little flymarks of black magic, or any familiars
   Such as mice or beetles which might preach
   Demonology in your skirting-board.
   I have wiped my shoes so that I shouldn't bring in
   The soft Egyptian sand which drifts at night,
   They tell me, into the corners of my house
   And then with the approach of naked morning
   Flies into the fire like a shadow of goldfinches.
   The tales unbelievable, the wild
   Tales they tell!
TYSON.   This will be discussed
   At the proper time——
THOMAS.   When we have finished talking
   About my murders.
MARGARET.   O peaceful and placid heaven,
   Are they both asking to be punished? Has death
   Become the fashionable way to live?
   Nothing would surprise me in their generation.

[24]

JENNET. Asking to be punished? Why, no, I have come
   Here to have the protection of your laughter.
   They accuse me of such a brainstorm of absurdities
   That all my fear dissolves in the humour of it.
   If I could perform what they say I *can* perform
   I should have got safely away from here
   As fast as you bat your eyelid.
TYSON.   Oh, indeed;
   Could you indeed?
JENNET.   They say I have only
   To crack a twig, and over the springtime weathercocks
   Cloudburst, hail and gale, whatever you will,
   Come leaping fury-foremost.
TYSON.   The report
   May be exaggerated, of course, but where there's smoke . . .
JENNET. They also say that I bring back the past;
   For instance, Helen comes,
   Brushing the maggots from her eyes,
   And, clearing her throat of several thousand years,
   She says 'I loved . . .'; but cannot any longer
   Remember names. Sad Helen. Or Alexander, wearing
   His imperial cobwebs and breastplate of shining worms
   Wakens and looks for his glasses, to find the empire
   Which he knows he put beside his bed.
TYSON. Whatever you say will be taken down in evidence
   Against you; am I making myself clear?
JENNET. They tell one tale that once, when the moon
   Was gibbous and in a high dazed state
   Of nimbus love, I shook a jonquil's dew
   On to a pearl and let a cricket chirp
   Three times, thinking of pale Peter:
   And there Titania was, vexed by a cloud
   Of pollen, using the sting of a bee to clean

[25]

Her nails and singing, as drearily as a gnat,
'Why try to keep clean?'

THOMAS.   'The earth is all of earth'—
                       So sang the queen:
                       So the queen sung,
              Crumbling her crownet into clods of dung.

JENNET. You heard her, too, Captain? Bravo. Is that
   A world you've got there, hidden under your hat?

THOMAS. Bedlam, ma'am, and the battlefield
   Uncle Adam died on. He was shot
   To bits with the core of an apple
   Which some fool of a serpent in the artillery
   Had shoved into God's cannon.

TYSON.   That's enough!
   Terrible frivolity, terrible blasphemy,
   Awful unorthodoxy. I can't understand
   Anything that is being said. Fetch a constable.
   The woman's tongue clearly knows the flavour
   Of *spiritu maligno*. The man must be
   Drummed out of the town.

THOMAS.   Oh, *must* he be?

RICHARD. Are you certain, sir? The constable? The lady
   Was laughing. She laughed at the very idea
   Of being a witch, sir.

TYSON.   Yes, just it, just it.
   Giving us a rigmarole of her dreams:
   Probably dreams: but intentionally
   Recollected, intentionally consented to,
   Intentionally delighted in. And so
   As dangerous as the act. Fetch the constable.

NICHOLAS. Sad, how things always are. We get one gulp
   Of dubious air from our hellmost origins

[26]

And we have to bung up the draught with a constable.
It's a terribly decontaminating life.

TYSON. I'll not have any frivolity. The town
Goes in terror.

MARGARET.   Sin is so inconvenient.

ALIZON. She is lovely. She is certain to be good.

TYSON. I have told you, Richard, twice, what to do.
Are you going about it?

RICHARD.   No, sir. Not yet.

TYSON. Did you speak to me? Now be careful how you answer.

JENNET. Can you be serious? I am Jennet Jourdemayne
And I believe in the human mind. Why play with me
And make me afraid of you, as you did for a moment,
I confess it. You can't believe—oh, surely, not
When the centuries of the world are piled so high—
You'll not believe what, in their innocence,
Those old credulous children in the street
Imagine of me?

THOMAS.   Innocence! Dear girl,
Before the world was, innocence
Was beaten by a lion all round the town.
And liked it.

JENNET.   What, does everyone still knuckle
And suckle at the big breast of irrational fears?
Do they really think I charm a sweat from Tagus,
Or lure an Amazonian gnat to fasten
On William Brown and shake him till he rattles?
Can they think and then think like this?

TYSON.   Will be
Gone into at the proper time. Disturbing
The peace. In every way. Have to arrest you.

JENNET. No!

[27]

THOMAS.   You bubble-mouthing, fog-blathering,
     Chin-chuntering, chap-flapping, liturgical,
     Turgidical, base old man! What about my murders?
     And what goes round in *your* head,
     What funny little murders and fornications
     Chatting up and down in three-four time
     Afraid to come out? What bliss to sin by proxy
     And do penance by way of someone else!
     But we'll not talk about you. It will make the outlook
     So dark. Neither about this exquisitely
     Mad young woman. Nor about this congenital
     Generator, your nephew here;
     Nor about anyone but me. I'm due
     To be hanged. Good Lord, aren't two murders enough
     To win me the medals of damnation? Must I put
     Half a dozen children on a spit
     And toast them at the flame that comes out of my mouth?
     You let the fairies fox you while the devil
     Does you. Concentrate on me.
TYSON.   I'll not
     Have it—I'll—I'll——
THOMAS.   Power of Job!
     Must I wait for a stammer? Your life, sir, is propelled
     By a dream of the fear of having nightmares; your love
     Is the fear of your single self; your world's history
     The fear of a possible leap by a possible antagonist
     Out of a possible shadow, or a not-improbable
     Skeleton out of your dead-certain cupboard.
     But here am I, the true phenomenon
     Of acknowledged guilt, steaming with the blood
     Of the pimp and the rag-and-bone man, Crime
     Transparent. What the hell are we waiting for?

[28]

TYSON. Will you attend to me? Will you be silent?

JENNET. Are you doing this to save me?

THOMAS.   You flatter my powers,
My sweet; you're too much a woman. But if you wish
You can go down to the dinner of damnation
On my arm.

JENNET.   I dine elsewhere.

TYSON.   Am I invisible?
Am I inaudible? Do I merely festoon
The room with my presence? Richard, wretched boy,
If you don't wish to incur considerable punishment
Do yourself the kindness to fetch the constable.
I don't care for these unexpurgated persons.
I shall lose my patience.

MARGARET.   I shall lose my faith
In the good-breeding of providence. Wouldn't this happen
Now: to-day: within an hour or two
Of everyone coming to congratulate
Humphrey and Alizon. Arrangements were made
A month ago, long before this gentleman's
Murders were even thought of.

TYSON.   They don't exist,
I say——

Enter HUMPHREY.

HUMPHREY. Uncle, there's a sizable rumpus,
Without exaggeration a how-do-you-do
Taking place in the street. I thought you should know.

TYSON. Rumpus?

HUMPHREY.   Perhaps rumpus isn't the word.
A minor kind of bloody revolution.
It's this damned rascal, this half-pay half-wit.
I should say he's certifiable. It seems

[29]

He's been spreading all around the town some tale
About drowning a pimp and murdering old Skipps
The rag-and-bone man.

THOMAS. Ah, old Skipps, old Skipps,
What a surplus of bones you'll have where you've gone to
now!

JENNET. Old Skipps? But he's the man——

TYSON. Will you both be silent?
I won't have every Tom, Dick, and Harry
Laying information against himself before
He's got written authority from me.

HUMPHREY. Quite right.
As it is, the town is hell's delight. They've looked
For the drowned pimp and they've looked for Skipps
And they've looked in the places where he says he left them
And they can't find either.

NICHOLAS. Can't find either?

HUMPHREY. Can't find either.

MARGARET. Of course they can't. When he first
Mentioned murders I knew he had got hold
Of a quite wrong end of the stick.

HUMPHREY. They say he's the Devil.

MARGARET. I can imagine who started *that* story.

HUMPHREY. But are we so sure he isn't? Outside in the street
They're convinced he's the Devil. And none of us ever having
Seen the Devil, how can we know? They say
He killed the old men and spirited them into the Limbo.
We can't search there. I don't even know where it is.

THOMAS. Sir, it's between me and the deep blue sea.
The wind of conscience blows straight from its plains.

HUMPHREY. Shut up.—If you're the Devil I beg your pardon.—

[30]

They also have the idea
He's got a girl in his toils, a witch called——
JENNET.   Jennet.
I am she.
HUMPHREY. God.
TYSON.   Well, Humphrey, well?
Is that the end of your information?
NICHOLAS.   Humphrey,
Have you spoken to your little future wife
Lately?
THOMAS. Tinder, easy tinder.
HUMPHREY.   In fact—
In fact——
NICHOLAS.   In fact it's all a bloody revolution.
TYSON. I'm being played with, I'm sure of it; something tells
    me
There is irresponsibility somewhere. Richard,
You'll not get out of this lightly. Where's the constable?
Why isn't he standing before me?
RICHARD.   I can see
No need for the constable, sir.
TYSON.   No need? No need?

Enter the CHAPLAIN *with his viol.*

CHAPLAIN. I am late for prayers, I know; I know you think
    me
A broken reed, and my instrument too, my better half,
You lacked it, I'm afraid. But life has such
Diversity, I sometimes remarkably lose
Eternity in the passing moment. Just now
In the street there's a certain boisterous interest
In a spiritual matter. They say——

TYSON.   I know what they say.

CHAPLAIN. Ah yes; you know. Sin, as well as God,
Moves in a most mysterious way. It is hard to imagine
Why the poor girl should turn Skipps into a dog.

NICHOLAS. Skipps? Skipps into a dog?

HUMPHREY.   But Skipps——

THOMAS. Skipps trundles in another place, calling
His raga-boa in gutters without end,
Transfigured by the spatial light
Of Garbage Indestructible. And I
Ought to know since I sent him there. A dog?
Come, come; don't let's be fanciful.

TYSON. They say one thing and another thing and both at
once;
I don't know. It will all have to be gone into
At the proper time——

HUMPHREY.   But this is a contradiction——

CHAPLAIN. Ah, isn't that life all over? And is this
The young assassin? If he is the doer of the damage
Can it be she also? My flock are employing
Fisticuffs over this very question.

HUMPHREY. But if he could be the Devil——

THOMAS.   Good boy! Shall I set
Your minds at rest and give you proof? Come here.

                    [*He whispers in* HUMPHREY's *ear.*

HUMPHREY. That's not funny.

THOMAS.   Not funny for the goats.

HUMPHREY. I've heard it before. He says the Day of Judgement
Is fixed for to-night.

MARGARET.   Oh no. I have always been sure
That when it comes it will come in the autumn.

[32]

Heaven, I am quite sure, wouldn't disappoint
The bulbs.

THOMAS.   Consider: vastiness lusted, mother;
A huge heaving desire, overwhelming solitude,
And the mountain belly of Time laboured
And brought forth man, the mouse. The spheres churned on,
Hoping to charm our ears
With sufficient organ-music, sadly sent out
On the wrong wave of sound; but still they roll
Fabulous and fine, a roundabout
Of doomed and golden notes. And on beyond,
Profound with thunder of oceanic power,
Lie the morose dynamics of our dumb friend
Jehovah.
Why should these omnipotent bombinations
Go on with the deadly human anecdote, which
From the first was never more than remotely funny?
No; the time has come for tombs to tip
Their refuse; for the involving ivy, the briar,
The convolutions of convolvulus,
To disentangle and make way
For the last great ascendancy of dust,
Sucked into judgement by a cosmic yawn
Of boredom. The Last Trump
Is timed for twenty-two forty hours precisely.

TYSON. This will all be gone into at the proper——

THOMAS.   Time
Will soon be most improper. Why not hang me
Before it's too late?

MARGARET.   I shall go and change my dress;
Then I shall both be ready for our guests
And whatever else may come upon the world.

[33]

HUMPHREY. I'm sure he's mad.

CHAPLAIN.   And his information, of course,
Is in opposition to what we are plainly told
In the Scriptures: that the hour will come——

NICHOLAS.   Do you think
He means it? I've an idea he's up to something
None of us knows about, not one of us.

ALIZON [*who has found her way to* RICHARD]. Quiet Richard,
son of nobody.

RICHARD [*whispering*]. It isn't always like this, I promise it
isn't.

JENNET. May I, Jennet Jourdemayne, the daughter
Of a man who believed the universe was governed
By certain laws, be allowed to speak?
Here is such a storm of superstition
And humbug and curious passions, where will you start
To look for the truth? Am I in fact
An enchantress bemused into collaboration
With the enemy of man? Is this the enemy,
This eccentric young gentleman never seen by me
Before? I say I am not. He says perhaps
He is. You say I am. You say he is not.
And now the eccentric young gentleman threatens us all
With imminent cataclysm. If, as a living creature,
I wish in all good faith to continue living,
Where do you suggest I should lodge my application?

TYSON. That is perfectly clear. You are both under arrest.

THOMAS. Into Pandora's box with all the ills.
But not if that little hell-cat Hope's
Already in possession. I've hoped enough.
I gave the best years of my life to that girl,
But I'm walking out with Damnation now, and she's
A flame who's got finality.

[34]

JENNET. Do you want no hope for me either? No compassion
   To lift suspicion off me?

THOMAS.   Lift? Compassion
   Has a rupture, lady. To hell with lifting.

JENNET. Listen, please listen to me!

THOMAS.   Let the world
   Go, lady; it isn't worth the candle.

TYSON. Take her, Richard; down to the cellars.

THOMAS.   You see?
   He has the key to every perplexity.
   Kiss your illusions for me before they go.

JENNET. But what will happen?

THOMAS. That's something even old nosedrip doesn't know.

                        [RICHARD *leads* JENNET *away.*

TYSON. Take him away!

THOMAS.   Mr. Mayor, hang me for pity's sake,
   For God's sake hang me, before I love that woman!

CURTAIN ON ACT ONE

[35]

Act Two

The same room, about an hour later. The CHAPLAIN *in a chair, sleeping.* TYSON *surrounded with papers.* EDWARD TAPPER-COOM, *the town's Justice, mountainously rolling up and down the room.*

TAPPERCOOM. Well, it's poss-ss-ible, it's poss-ss-ible.
I *may* have been putting the Devil to the torture.
But can you smell scorching?—not a singe
For my sins—that's from yesterday: I leaned
Across a candle. For all practical purposes
I feel as unblasted as on the day I was born.
And God knows I'm a target. Cupid scarcely
Needs to aim, and no devil could miss me.

TYSON. But his action may be delayed. We really must
Feel our way. We don't want to put ourselves wrong
With anything as positive as evil.

TAPPERCOOM. We have put him to the merest thumbscrew, Tyson,
Courteously and impartially, the purest
Cajolery to coax him to deny
These cock-and-bull murders for which there isn't a scrap
Of evidence.

TYSON.   Ah; ah. How does he take it?
Has he denied them?

TAPPERCOOM.   On the contrary.
He says he has also committed petty larceny,
Abaction, peculation and incendiarism.
As for the woman Jourdemayne——

TYSON.   Ah, yes,

[36]

Jourdemayne; what are we to make of her?
Wealthy, they tell me. But on the other hand
Quite affectingly handsome. Sad, you know.
We see where the eye can't come, eh, Tappercoom?
And all's not glorious within; no use
Saying it is.—I had a handkerchief.
Ah yes; buried amongst all this evidence.

TAPPERCOOM. Now, no poetics, Tyson. Blow your nose
And avoid lechery. Keep your eye on the evidence
Against her; there's plenty of it there. Religion
Has made an honest woman of the supernatural
And we won't have it kicking over the traces again,
Will we, Chaplain?—In the Land of Nod.
Admirable man.

TYSON.   Humanity,
That's all, Tappercoom; it's perfectly proper.
No one is going to let it interfere
With anything serious. I use it with great
Discretion, I assure you.—Has she confessed?

TAPPERCOOM. Not at all. Though we administer persuasion
With great patience, she admits nothing. And the man
Won't stop admitting. It really makes one lose
All faith in human nature.

Enter MARGARET, *without her placidity.*

MARGARET.   Who has the tongs?
The tongs, Hebble, the tongs, dear! Sweet
Elijah, we shall all go up in flames!

TYSON. Flames? Did you hear that, Tappercoom? Flames!
My sister said flames!

MARGARET.   A log the size of a cheese
Has fallen off the fire! Well, where are they?
What men of action! Tongs, I said!—Chaplain,

[37]

They're under your feet. Very simple you'd look
As a pile of ashes.

[*Exit.*

TYSON.   Oh. I beg your pardon,
Tappercoom. A blazing log.
CHAPLAIN.   Would there be something
I could do? I was asleep, you know.
TYSON. All this evidence from the witchfinder. . . .
TAPPERCOOM. The advent of a woman cannot be
Too gradual. I am not a nervous man
But I like to be predisposed to an order of events.
CHAPLAIN. It was very interesting: I was dreaming I stood
On Jacob's ladder, waiting for the Gates to open.
And the ladder was made entirely of diminished sevenths.
I was surprised but not put out. Nothing
Is altogether what we suppose it to be.
TAPPERCOOM. As for the Day of Judgement, we can be sure
It's not due yet. What are we told the world
Will be like? 'Boasters, blasphemers, without natural
Affection, traitors, trucebreakers,' and the rest of it.
Come, we've still a lot of backsliding ahead of us.
TYSON. Are you uneasy, Tappercoom?
TAPPERCOOM.   No, Tyson.
The whole thing's a lot of amphigourious
Stultiloquential fiddle-faddle.

Re-enter MARGARET, *head-first.*

MARGARET.   Hebble!
TAPPERCOOM. For God's sake!
TYSON.   What is it now? What is it?
MARGARET. The street's gone mad. They've seen a shooting
star!
TYSON. They? Who? What of it?

[38]

MARGARET.   I'm sure I'm sorry,
But the number of people gone mad in the street
Is particularly excessive. They were shaking
Our gate, and knocking off each other's hats
And six fights simultaneously, and some
Were singing psalm a hundred and forty—I think
It's a hundred and forty—and the rest of them shouting
'The Devil's in there!' (pointing at this house)
'Safety from Satan!' and 'Where's the woman? Where's
The witch? Send her out!'; and using words
That are only fit for the Bible. And I'm sure
There was blood in the gutter from somebody's head
Or else it was the sunset in a puddle,
But Jobby Pinnock was prising up cobblestones,
Roaring like the north wind, and you know
What he is in church when he starts on the responses.
And that old Habbakuk Brown using our wall
As it was never meant to be used. And then
They saw the star fall over our roof somewhere
And followed its course with a downrush of whistling
And Ohs and Ahs and groans and screams; and Jobby
Pinnock dropped a stone on his own foot
And roared 'Almighty God, it's a sign!' and some
Went down on their knees and others fell over them
And they've started to fight again, and the hundred and
    fortieth
Psalm has begun again louder and faster than ever.
Hebble dear, isn't it time they went home?
TYSON. All right, yes, all right, all right. Now why
Can't people mind their own business? This shooting star
Has got nothing to do with us, I am quite happy
In my mind about that. It probably went past
Perfectly preoccupied with some astral anxiety or other

[39]

Without giving us a second thought. Eh, Tappercoom?
One of those quaint astrological holus-boluses,
Quite all right.

TAPPERCOOM.   Quite. An excess of phlegm
In the solar system. It was on its way
To a heavenly spittoon. How is that,
How is that? On its way——

TYSON.   I consider it unwise
To tempt providence with humour, Tappercoom.

MARGARET. And on the one evening when we expect company!
What company is going to venture to get here
Through all that heathen hullabaloo in the road?
Except the glorious company of the Apostles,
And we haven't enough glasses for all that number.

TAPPERCOOM. Doomsday or not, we must keep our integrity.
We cannot set up dangerous precedents
Of speed. We shall sincerely hope, of course,
That Doomsday will refrain from precipitous action;
But the way we have gone must be the way we arrive.

CHAPLAIN. I wish I were a thinking man, very much.
Of course I feel a good deal, but that's no help to you.

TYSON. I'm not bewildered, I assure you I'm not
Bewildered. As a matter of fact a plan
Is almost certainly forming itself in my head
At this very moment. It may even be adequate.

CHAPLAIN. Where did I put my better half? I laid it
Aside. I could take it down to the gate and perhaps
Disperse them with a skirmish or two of the bow.
Orpheus, you know, was very successful in that way,
But of course I haven't his talent, not nearly his talent.

TYSON. If you would allow me to follow my train of
    thought——

[40]

TAPPERCOOM. It's my belief the woman Jourdemayne
Got hold of the male prisoner by unlawful
Supernatural soliciting
And bewitched him into a confession of murder
To draw attention away from herself. But the more
We coax him to withdraw his confession, the more
Crimes he confesses to.

CHAPLAIN.   I know I am not
A practical person; legal matters and so forth
Are Greek to me, except, of course,
That I understand Greek. And what may seem nonsensical
To men of affairs like yourselves might not seem so
To me, since everything astonishes me,
Myself most of all. When I think of myself
I can scarcely believe my senses. But there it is,
All my friends tell me I actually exist
And by an act of faith I have come to believe them.
But this fellow who is being such a trouble to us,
He, on the contrary, is so convinced
He *is* that he wishes he was NOT. Now why
Should that be?

TAPPERCOOM.   I believe you mean to tell us,
Chaplain.

MARGARET. I might as well sit down, for all
The good that standing up does.

CHAPLAIN.   I imagine
He finds the world not entirely salubrious.
If he cannot be stayed with flagons, or comforted
With apples—I quote, of course—or the light, the ocean,
The ever-changing . . . I mean and stars, extraordinary
How many, or some instrument or other—I am afraid
I appear rhapsodical—but perhaps the addition
Of your thumbscrew will not succeed either. The point

[41]

I'm attempting to make is this one: he might be wooed
From his aptitude for death by being happier;
And what I was going to suggest, quite irresponsibly,
Is that he might be invited to partake
Of our festivities this evening. No,
I see it astonishes you.

MARGARET.   Do you mean ask him——

TYSON. I have heard very little of what you have said, Chaplain,
Being concerned, as I am, with a certain Thought,
But am I to believe that you recommend our inviting
This undesirable character to rub shoulders
With my sister?

CHAPLAIN.   Ah; rubbing shoulders. I hadn't exactly
Anticipated that. It was really in relation to the soul
That the possibility crossed my mind——

TAPPERCOOM. As a criminal the boy is a liability.
I doubt very much if he could supply a farthing
Towards the cost of his execution. So
You suggest, Chaplain, we let him bibulate
From glass to glass this evening, help him to
A denial of his guilt and get him off our hands
Before daybreak gets the town on its feet again?

MARGARET. I wish I could like the look of the immediate
Future, but I don't.

TYSON.   I'm glad to tell you
An idea has formed in my mind, a possible solution.

Enter RICHARD.

RICHARD. Sir, if you please——

TYSON.   Well, Richard?

RICHARD.   I should like to admit
That I've drunk some of the wine put out for the guests.

TYSON. Well, that's a pretty thing, I must say.

[42]

RICHARD.   I was feeling
    Low; abominably; about the prisoners,
    And the row in the street that's getting out of hand—
    And certain inner things. And I saw the wine
    And I thought Well, here goes, and I drank
    Three glassesful.

TYSON.   I trust you feel better for it.

RICHARD. I feel much worse. Those two, sir, the prisoners,
    What are you doing with them? I don't know why
    I keep calling you Sir. I'm not feeling respectful.
    If only inflicted pain could be as contagious
    As a plague, you might use it more sparingly.

TAPPERCOOM. Who's this cub of a boy?

MARGARET.   Richard, be sensible.
    He's a dear boy but a green boy, and I'm sure
    He'll apologize in a minute or two.

TYSON.   The boy
    Is a silly boy, he's a silly boy; and I'm going
    To punish him.

MARGARET.   Where are Humphrey and Nicholas?

TYSON. Now, Margaret——

RICHARD.   They were where the prisoners are,
    Down in the cellars.

MARGARET.   Not talking to that witch?

RICHARD. There isn't a witch. They were sitting about on bar-
    rels.
    It seemed that neither would speak while the other was there
    And neither would go away. Half an hour ago.
    They may be there still.

TYSON.   I must remind you, Margaret,
    I was speaking to this very stupid boy.
    He is going to scrub the floor. Yes, scrub it.
    Scrub this floor this evening before our guests

[43]

Put in an appearance. Mulish tasks for a mulish
Fellow. I haven't forgotten his refusal
To fetch the constable.

RICHARD.   Has Alizon Eliot
Been left sitting alone?

MARGARET.   Alizon Eliot
Is not for you to be concerned with, Richard.

TYSON. Am I supposed to be merely exercising my tongue
Or am I being listened to? Do you hear me?

RICHARD. Yes; scrub the floor.—No, she is not;
I know that.

TYSON.   Furthermore, you'll relegate
Yourself to the kitchen to-night, fetching and carrying.
If you wish to be a mule you shall be a mule.

                    [*He hands* RICHARD *a note.*
And take this to whatever splendid fellow's
On duty. You will return with the prisoners
And tell them to remain in this room till I send for them.
—Tactics, Tappercoom: the idea that came to me.
You'll think it very good.—You may go, Richard.

                              [*Exit* RICHARD.

TAPPERCOOM. I am nothing but the Justice here, of course,
But, perhaps, even allowing for that, you could tell me
What the devil you're up to.

Enter NICHOLAS *with a gash on his forehead, followed more
                    slowly by* HUMPHREY.

NICHOLAS.   Look, Chaplain: blood.
Fee, fi, fo, fum. Can you smell it?

MARGARET. Now what have you been doing?

NICHOLAS.   Isn't it beautiful?
A splash from the cherry-red river that drives my mill!

[44]

CHAPLAIN. Well, yes, it has a cheerful appearance,
But isn't it painful?

MARGARET.   I am sure it's painful.
How did you——

HUMPHREY.   Mother, I make it known publicly:
I'm tired of my little brother. Will you please
Give him to some charity?

NICHOLAS.   Give me to faith
And hope and the revolution of our native town.
I've been hit on the head by two-thirds of a brick.

HUMPHREY. The young fool climbed on the wall and ad-
dressed the crowd.

NICHOLAS. They were getting discouraged. I told them how
happy it made me
To see them interested in world affairs
And how the conquest of evil was being openly
Discussed in this house at that very moment
And then unfortunately I was hit by a brick.

MARGARET. What in the world have world affairs
To do with anything? But we won't argue.

TYSON. I believe that brick to have been divinely delivered,
And richly deserved. And am I to understand
You boys have also attempted conversation
With the prisoners?

HUMPHREY.   Now surely, uncle,
As one of the Town Council I should be allowed
To get a grasp of whatever concerns the welfare
Of the population? Nicholas, I agree,
Had no business on earth to be down there.

NICHOLAS.   I was on
Business of the soul, my sweetheart, business
Of the soul.

[45]

MARGARET.   You may use that word once too often,
Nicholas. Heaven or someone will take you seriously
And then you *would* look foolish. Come with me
And have your forehead seen to.

NICHOLAS.   But my big brother
Was on business of the flesh, by all the fires
Of Venus, weren't you, Humphrey?

HUMPHREY.   What the hell
Do you mean by that, you little death-watch beetle?

MARGARET. Nicholas, will you come?

NICHOLAS.   Certainly, mother.

[*Exit* MARGARET *and* NICHOLAS.

TYSON. How very remarkably insufferable
Young fellows can sometimes be. One would expect them
To care to model themselves on riper minds
Such as our own, Tappercoom. But really
We might as well have not existed, you know.

TAPPERCOOM. Am I to hear your plan, Tyson, or am I
Just to look quietly forward to old age?

TYSON. My plan, ah, yes. Conclusive and humane.
The two are brought together into this room.—
How does that strike you?

TAPPERCOOM.   It makes a complete sentence:
Subject: they. Predicate: are brought together——

TYSON. Ah, you will say 'with what object?' I'll tell you. We,
That is: ourselves, the Chaplain, and my elder nephew—
Will remain unobserved in the adjoining room
With the communicating door ajar.—And how
Does that strike you?

TAPPERCOOM.   With a dull thud, Tyson,
If I may say so.

TYSON.   I see the idea has eluded you.
A hypothetical Devil, Tappercoom,

[46]

Brought into conversation with a witch.
A dialogue of Hell, perhaps, and conclusive.
Or one or other by their exchange of words
Will prove to be innocent, or we shall have proof
Positive of guilt. Does that seem good?

TAPPERCOOM. Good is as good results.

HUMPHREY.   I should never have thought
You would have done anything so undignified
As to stoop to keyholes, uncle.

TYSON.   No, no, no.
The door will be ajar, my boy.

HUMPHREY.   Ah yes,
That will make us upright.—I can hear them coming.

TYSON [going]. Come along, come along.

CHAPLAIN.   'The ears of them that hear
Shall hearken.' The prophet Isaiah.

TYSON.   Come along, Chaplain.

TAPPERCOOM [following]. A drink, Tyson. I wish to slake
the dryness
Of my disbelief.

                              [They go in. The CHAPLAIN returns.

CHAPLAIN.   I mustn't leave my mistress.
Where are you, angel? Just where chucklehead left her.

Enter RICHARD *with* JENNET *and* THOMAS.

RICHARD. He wants you to wait here till he sends for you.
If in some way—I wish—! I must fetch the scrubbers.
                              [Exit RICHARD.

CHAPLAIN. Ah . . . ah . . . I'm not really here. I came
For my angel, a foolish way to speak of it,
This instrument. May I say, a happy issue
Out of all your afflictions? I hope so.—Well,
I'm away now.

[47]

THOMAS. God bless you, in case you sneeze.

CHAPLAIN. Yes; thank you. I may. And God bless you.

[*Exit* CHAPLAIN.

THOMAS [*at the window*]. You would think by the holy scent
of it our friend
Had been baptizing the garden. But it's only
The heathen rainfall.

JENNET. Do you think he knows
What has been happening to us?

THOMAS. Old angel-scraper?
He knows all right. But he's subdued
To the cloth he works in.

JENNET. How tired I am.

THOMAS. And palingenesis has come again
With a hey and a ho. The indomitable
Perseverance of Persephone
Became ludicrous long ago.

JENNET. What can you see
Out there?

THOMAS. Out here? Out here is a sky so gentle
Five stars are ventured on it. I can see
The sky's pale belly glowing and growing big,
Soon to deliver the moon. And I can see
A glittering smear, the snail-trail of the sun
Where it crawled with its golden shell into the hills.
A darkening land sunken into prayer
Lucidly in dewdrops of one syllable,
Nunc dimittis. I see twilight, madam.

JENNET. But what can you hear?

THOMAS. The howl of human jackals.

Enter RICHARD *with pail and scrubbing-brush.*

RICHARD. Do you mind? I have to scrub the floor.

[48]

THOMAS. A good old custom. Always fornicate
    Between clean sheets and spit on a well-scrubbed floor.
JENNET. Twilight, double, treble, in and out!
    If I try to find my way I bark my brain
    On shadows sharp as rocks where half a day
    Ago was a wild soft world, a world of warm
    Straw, whispering every now and then
    With rats, but possible, possible, not this,
    This where I'm lost. The morning came, and left
    The sunlight on my step like any normal
    Tradesman. But now every spark
    Of likelihood has gone. The light draws off
    As easily as though no one could die
    To-morrow.
THOMAS.   Are you going to be so serious
    About such a mean allowance of breath as life is?
    We'll suppose ourselves to be caddis-flies
    Who live one day. Do we waste the evening
    Commiserating with each other about
    The unhygienic condition of our worm-cases?
    For God's sake, shall we laugh?
JENNET.   For what reason?
THOMAS. For the reason of laughter, since laughter is surely
    The surest touch of genius in creation.
    Would *you* ever have thought of it, I ask you,
    If you had been making man, stuffing him full
    Of such hopping greeds and passions that he has
    To blow himself to pieces as often as he
    Conveniently can manage it—would it also
    Have occurred to you to make him burst himself
    With such a phenomenon as cachinnation?
    That same laughter, madam, is an irrelevancy
    Which almost amounts to revelation.

[49]

JENNET.   I laughed
    Earlier this evening, and where am I now?

THOMAS.   Between
    The past and the future which is where you were
    Before.

JENNET. Was it for laughter's sake you told them
    You were the Devil? Or why did you?

THOMAS.   Honesty,
    Madam, common honesty.

JENNET.   Honesty common
    With the Devil?

THOMAS.   Gloriously common. It's Evil, for once
    Not travelling incognito. It is what it is,
    The Great Unspurious.

JENNET.   Thank you for that.
    You speak of the world I thought I was waking to
    This morning. But horror is walking round me here
    Because nothing is as it appears to be.
    That's the deep water my childhood had to swim in.
    My father was drowned in it.

THOMAS.   He was drowned in what?
    In hypocrisy?

JENNET.   In the pursuit of alchemy.
    In refusing to accept your dictum 'It is
    What it is.' Poor father. In the end he walked
    In Science like the densest night. And yet
    He was greatly gifted.
    When he was born he gave an algebraic
    Cry; at one glance measured the cubic content
    Of that ivory cone his mother's breast
    And multiplied his appetite by five.
    So he matured by a progression, gained
    Experience by correlation, expanded

[50]

Into a marriage by contraction, and by
Certain physical dynamics
Formulated me. And on he went
Still deeper into the calculating twilight
Under the twinkling of five-pointed figures
Till Truth became for him the sum of sums
And Death the long division. My poor father.
What years and powers he wasted.
He thought he could change the matter of the world
From the poles to the simultaneous equator
By strange experiment and by describing
Numerical parabolas.

THOMAS.   To change
The matter of the world! Magnificent
Intention. And so he died deluded.

JENNET. As a matter of fact, it wasn't a delusion.
As a matter of fact, after his death
When I was dusting the laboratory
I knocked over a crucible which knocked
Over another which rocked a third, and they poured
And spattered over some copper coins which two days later
By impregnation had turned into solid gold.

THOMAS. Tell that to some sailor on a horse!
If you had such a secret, I
And all my fiendish flock, my incubi,
Succubi, imps and cacodemons, would have leapt
Out of our bath of brimming brimstone, crying
Eureka, cherchez la femme!—Emperors
Would be colonizing you, their mistresses
Patronizing you, ministers of state
Governmentalizing you. And you
Would be eulogized, lionized, probably
Canonized for your divine mishap.

[51]

JENNET. But I never had such a secret. It's a secret
Still. What it was I spilt, or to what extent,
Or in what proportion; whether the atmosphere
Was hot, cold, moist or dry, I've never known.
And someone else can discolour their fingers, tease
Their brains and spoil their eyesight to discover it.
My father broke on the wheel of a dream; he was lost
In a search. And so, for me, the actual!
What I touch, what I see, what I know; the essential fact.

THOMAS. In other words, the bare untruth.

JENNET.   And, if I may say it
Without appearing rude, absolutely
No devils.

THOMAS.   How in the miserable world, in that case,
Do you come to be here, pursued by the local consignment
Of fear and guilt? What possible cause——

JENNET.   Your thumbs.
I'm sure they're giving you pain.

THOMAS.   Listen! by both
My cloven hooves! if you put us to the rack
Of an exchange of sympathy, I'll fell you to the ground.
Answer my question.

JENNET.   Why do they call me a witch?
Remember my father was an alchemist.
I live alone, preferring loneliness
To the companionable suffocation of an aunt.
I still amuse myself with simple experiments
In my father's laboratory. Also I speak
French to my poodle. Then you must know
I have a peacock which on Sundays
Dines with me indoors. Not long ago
A new little serving maid carrying the food
Heard its cry, dropped everything and ran,

[52]

Never to come back, and told all whom she met
That the Devil was dining with me.

THOMAS.   It really is
Beyond the limit of respectable superstition
To confuse my voice with a peacock's. Don't they know
I sing solo bass in Hell's Madrigal Club?
—And as for you, you with no eyes, no ears,
No senses, you the most superstitious
Of all—(for what greater superstition
Is there than the mumbo-jumbo of believing
In reality?)—you should be swallowed whole by Time
In the way that you swallow appearances.
Horns, what a waste of effort it has been
To give you Creation's vast and exquisite
Dilemma! where altercation thrums
In every granule of the Milky Way,
Persisting still in the dead-sleep of the moon,
And heckling itself hoarse in that hot-head
The sun. And as for here, each acorn drops
Arguing to earth, and pollen's all polemic.—
We have given you a world as contradictory
As a female, as cabbalistic as the male,
A conscienceless hermaphrodite who plays
Heaven off against hell, hell off against heaven,
Revolving in the ballroom of the skies
Glittering with conflict as with diamonds:
We have wasted paradox and mystery on you
When all you ask us for, is cause and effect!—
A copy of your birth-certificate was all you needed
To make you at peace with Creation. How uneconomical
The whole thing's been.

JENNET.   This is a fine time
To scold me for keeping myself to myself and out

[53]

Of the clutch of chaos. I was already
In a poor way of perplexity and now
You leave me no escape except
Out on a stream of tears.

THOMAS [*falling over* RICHARD *scrubbing*]. Now, none of
  that!—
  Hell!

RICHARD. I beg your pardon.

THOMAS.   Now that I'm down
  On my knees I may as well stay here. In the name
  Of all who ever were drowned at sea, don't weep!
  I never learnt to swim. May God keep you
  From being my Hellespont.

JENNET.   What I do
  With my own tears is for me to decide.

THOMAS. That's all very well. You get rid of them.
  But on whose defenceless head are they going to fall?

JENNET. I had no idea you were so afraid of water.
  I'll put them away.

THOMAS.   O Pete, I don't know which
  Is worse; to have you crying or to have you behaving
  Like Catharine of Aix, who never wept
  Until after she had been beheaded, and then
  The accumulation of the tears of a long lifetime
  Burst from her eyes with such force, they practic'ly winded
  Three onlookers and floated the parish priest
  Two hundred yards into the entrance-hall
  Of a brothel.

JENNET.   Poor Catharine!

THOMAS.   Not at all.
  It made her life in retrospect infinitely
  More tolerable, and when she got to Purgatory

[54]

She was laughing so much they had to give her a sedative. *laugh*

JENNET. Why should you want to be hanged?

THOMAS.   Madam, *loud*

I owe it to myself. But I can leave it *soft*
Until the last moment. It will keep
While the light still lasts. *and what is your (loud) mystery?*

JENNET.   What can we see in this light?

Nothing, I think, except flakes of drifting fear,
The promise of oblivion.

THOMAS.   Nothing can be seen
In the thistle-down, but the rough-head thistle comes.
Rest in that riddle. I can pass to you
Generations of roses in this wrinkled berry.
There: now you hold in your hand a race
Of summer gardens, it lies under centuries
Of petals. What is not, you have in your palm.
Rest in the riddle, rest; why not? This evening
Is a ridiculous wisp of down
Blowing in the air as disconsolately as dust.
And you have your own damnable mystery too,
Which at this moment I could well do without.

JENNET. I know of none. I'm an unhappy fact
Fearing death. This is a strange moment   *soft*
To feel my life increasing, when this moment   *high*
And a little more may be for both of us   *fast*
The end of time. You've cast your fishing-net
Of eccentricity, your seine of insanity
Caught me when I was already lost
And landed me with despairing gills on your own   *slow down*
Strange beach. That's too inhuman of you.

THOMAS.   Inhuman? *ingatii*

If I dared to know what you meant it would sound disastrous!

[55]

JENNET. It means I care whether you live or die.
You have cut yourself a shape on the air, which may be
My scar.

THOMAS.   Will you stop frightening me to death?
Do you want our spirits to hobble out of their graves
Enduring twinges of hopeless human affection
As long as death shall last? Still to suffer
Pain in the amputated limb! To feel
Passion *in vacuo!* That is the sort of thing
That causes sun-spots, and the lord knows what
Infirmities in the firmament. I tell you
The heart is worthless,
Nothing more than a pomander's perfume
In the sewerage. And a nosegay of private emotion
Won't distract me from the stench of the plague-pit,
You needn't think it will.—Excuse me, Richard.—
Don't entertain the mildest interest in me
Or you'll have me die screaming.

JENNET.   Why should that be?
If you're afraid of your shadow falling across
Another life, shine less brightly upon yourself,
Step back into the rank and file of men,
Instead of preserving the magnetism of mystery
And your curious passion for death. You are making yourself
A breeding-ground for love and must take the consequences.
But what are you afraid of, since in a little
While neither of us may exist? Either or both
May be altogether transmuted into memory,
And then the heart's obscure indeed.—Richard,
There's a tear rolling out of your eye. What is it?

RICHARD. Oh, that? I don't really know. I have things on my
mind.

JENNET. Not us?

[56]

RICHARD. Not only.

THOMAS.   If it's a woman, Richard,
Apply yourself to the scrubbing-brush. It's all
A trick of the light.

JENNET.   The light of a fire.

THOMAS. ~~Make this woman~~ understand that I   *can I not make*   ~~And Richard,~~ *And Richard, you woman*
Am a figure of vice and crime——   *deep feeling*

JENNET.   Guilty of——   *high*

THOMAS.   Guilty
Of mankind. I have perpetrated human nature.
My father and mother were accessaries before the fact,   *deep*
But there'll be no accessaries after the fact,   *fast*
By my virility there won't! Just see me   *! !*
As I am, me like a perambulating
Vegetable, patched with inconsequential   *low*
Hair, looking out of two small jellies for the means
Of life, balanced on folding bones, my sex
No beauty but a blemish to be hidden
Behind judicious rags, driven and scorched   *loud : !*
By boomerang rages and lunacies which never
Touch the accommodating artichoke   *low*
Or the seraphic strawberry beaming in its bed:
I defend myself against pain and death by pain
And death, and make the world go round, they tell me,   *loud*
By one of my less lethal appetites:
Half this grotesque life I spend in a state   *fast low*
Of slow decomposition, using
The name of unconsidered God as a pedestal   *loud*
On which I stand and bray that I'm best
Of beasts, until under some patient
Moon or other I fall to pieces, like   *low*

[57]

A cake of dung. Is there a slut would hold
This in her arms and put her lips against it?
JENNET. Sluts are only human. By a quirk
Of unastonished nature, your obscene
Decaying figure of vegetable fun
Can drag upon a woman's heart, as though
Heaven were dragging up the roots of hell.
What is to be done? Something compels us into
The terrible fallacy that man is desirable
And there's no escaping into truth. The crimes
And cruelties leave us longing, and campaigning
Love still pitches his tent of light among
The suns and moons. You may be decay and a platitude
Of flesh, but I have no other such memory of life.
You may be corrupt as ancient apples, well then
Corruption is what I most willingly harvest.
You are Evil, Hell, the Father of Lies; if so
Hell is my home and my days of good were a holiday:
Hell is my hill and the world slopes away from it
Into insignificance. I have come suddenly
Upon my heart and where it is I see no help for.
THOMAS. We're lost, both irretrievably lost——

Enter TYSON, TAPPERCOOM, HUMPHREY, *and the* CHAPLAIN.

TAPPERCOOM.   Certainly.
The woman has confessed. *Spargere auras*
Per vulgum ambiguas. The town can go to bed.
TYSON. It was a happy idea, eh, Tappercoom? This will be
A great relief to my sister, and everybody
Concerned. A very nice confession, my dear.
THOMAS. What is this popping-noise? Now what's the matter?
JENNET. Do they think I've confessed to witchcraft?
TAPPERCOOM.   Admirably.

[58]

CHAPLAIN [*to* JENNET]. Bother such sadness. You under-
  stand, I'm sure:
  Those in authority over us. I should like
  To have been a musician but others decreed otherwise.
  And sin, whatever we might prefer, cannot
  Go altogether unregarded.
TAPPERCOOM.   Now,
  Now, Chaplain, don't get out of hand.
  Pieties come later.—Young Devize
  Had better go and calm the populace.
  Tell them faggots will be lit to-morrow at noon.
HUMPHREY. Have a heart, Mr. Tappercoom; they're hurling
  bricks.
JENNET. What do they mean? Am I at noon to go
  To the fire? Oh, for pity! Why must they brand
  Themselves with me?
THOMAS.   She has bribed you to procure
  Her death! Graft! Graft! Oh, the corruption
  Of this town when only the rich can get to kingdom-
  Come and a poor man is left to groan
  In the full possession of his powers. And she's
  Not even guilty! I demand fair play
  For the criminal classes!
TYSON.   Terrible state of mind.
  Humphrey, go at once to the gate——
HUMPHREY.   Ah well, I can
  But try to dodge.
THOMAS [*knocking him down*]. You didn't try soon enough.
  Who else is going to cheat me out of my death?
  Whee, ecclesiastic, let me brain you
  With your wife!
          [*He snatches the* CHAPLAIN's *viol and offers to hit
          him on the head.*

[59]

CHAPLAIN.   No, no! With something else—oh, please
    Hit me with something else.
THOMAS.   Exchange it
    For a harp and hurry off to heaven.—Am I dangerous?
    Will you give me the gallows?—Now, *now*, Mr. Mayor!
    Richard, I'll drown him in your bucket.

                                    [JENNET *faints.*
RICHARD [*running to support her*]. Look, she has fallen!
CHAPLAIN.   Air! Air!
TYSON.   Water!
THOMAS. But no fire, do you hear? No fire!—How is she,
    Richard?
    Oh, the delicate mistiming of women! She has carefully
    Snapped in half my jawbone of an ass.
RICHARD. Life is coming back.
THOMAS.   Importunate life.
    It should have something better to do
    Than to hang about at a chronic street-corner
    In dirty weather and worse company.
TAPPERCOOM. It is my duty as Justice to deliver
    Sentence on you as well.
THOMAS.   Ah!
TAPPERCOOM.   Found guilty
    Of jaundice, misanthropy, suicidal tendencies
    And spreading gloom and despondency. You will spend
    The evening joyously, sociably, taking part
    In the pleasures of your fellow men.
THOMAS.   Not
    Until you've hanged me. I'll be amenable then.
JENNET. Have I come back to consciousness to hear
    That still?—Richard, help me to stand.—You see,
    Preacher to the caddis-fly, I return
    To live my allotted span of insect hours.

[60]

But if you batter my wings with talk of death
I'll drop to the ground again.

THOMAS.   Ah! One
Concession to your courage and then no more.
Gentlemen, I'll accept your most inhuman
Sentence. I'll not disturb the indolence
Of your gallows yet. But on one condition:
That this lady shall take her share to-night
Of awful festivity. She shall suffer too.

TYSON. Out of the question, quite out of the question,
Absolutely out of the question. What, what?

TAPPERCOOM. What?

THOMAS.   Then you shall spend your night in searching
For the bodies of my victims, or else the Lord
Chief Justice of England shall know you let a murderer
Go free. I'll raise the country.

JENNET.   Do you think
I can go in gaiety to-night
Under the threat of to-morrow? If I could sleep——

THOMAS. That is the heaven to come.
We should be like stars now that it's dark:
Use ourselves up to the last bright dregs
And vanish in the morning. Shall we not
Suffer as wittily as we can? Now, come,
Don't purse your lips like a little prude at the humour
Of annihilation. It is somewhat broad
I admit, but we're not children.

JENNET.   I am such
A girl of habit. I had got into the way
Of being alive. I will live as well as I can
This evening.

THOMAS.   And I'll live too, if it kills me.

[61]

HUMPHREY. Well, uncle? If you're going to let this clumsy-
Fisted cut-throat loose on the house to-night,
Why not the witch-girl, too?
CHAPLAIN.   Foolishly
I can't help saying it, I should like
To see them dancing.
TYSON. We have reached a decision.
The circumstances compel us to agree
To your most unorthodox request.
THOMAS.   Wisdom
At last. But listen, woman: after this evening
I have no further interest in the world.
JENNET. My interest also will not be great, I imagine,
After this evening.

CURTAIN ON ACT TWO

Act Three

*Later the same night. The same room, by torchlight and moon-
light.* HUMPHREY *at the window. Enter* THOMAS, *who
talks to himself until he notices* HUMPHREY.

THOMAS. O tedium, tedium, tedium. The frenzied
Ceremonial drumming of the humdrum!
Where in this small-talking world can I find
A longitude with no platitude?—I must
Apologize. That was no joke to be heard
Making to myself in the full face of the moon.
If only I had been born flame, a flame
Poised, say, on the flighty head of a candle,
I could have stood in this draught and gone out,
Whip, through the door of my exasperation.
But I remain, like the possibility
Of water in a desert.

HUMPHREY.   I'm sure nobody
Keeps you here. There's a road outside if you want it.

THOMAS. What on earth should I do with a road, that furrow
On the forehead of imbecility, a road?
I would as soon be up there, walking in the moon's
White unmolared gums. I'll sit on the world
And rotate with you till we roll into the morning.

HUMPHREY. You're a pestering parasite. If I had my way
You'd be got rid of. You're mad and you're violent,
And I strongly resent finding you slightly pleasant.

THOMAS. O God, yes, so do I.

Enter NICHOLAS.

[63]

NICHOLAS.   As things turn out
  I want to commit an offence.
THOMAS.   Does something prevent you?
NICHOLAS. I don't know what offence to commit.
THOMAS.   What abysmal
  Poverty of mind!
NICHOLAS.   This is a night
  Of the most asphyxiating enjoyment that ever
  Sapped my youth.
HUMPHREY.   I think I remember
  The stars gave you certain rights and interest
  In a little blonde religious. How is she, Nicholas?
NICHOLAS. Your future wife, Humphrey, if that is who
  You mean, is pale, tearful, and nibbling a walnut.
  I loved her once—earlier to-day—
  Loved her with a passionate misapprehension.
  I thought you wanted her, and I'm always deeply
  Devoted to your affairs. But now I'm bored,
  As bored as the face of a fish,
  In spite of the sunlit barley of her hair.
HUMPHREY. Aren't I ready to marry her? I thought that was
    why
  We were mooning around celebrating. What more
  Can I do to make you take her off my hands?
  And I'm more than ready for the Last Trump as well.
  It will stop old Mrs. Cartwright talking.
NICHOLAS.   Never.
  She's doom itself. She could talk a tombstone off anybody.

Enter MARGARET.

MARGARET. Oh, there you are. Whatever's wrong? You both
  Go wandering off, as though our guests could be gay
  Of their own accord (the few who could bring themselves
  [64]

To bring themselves, practically in the teeth
Of the recording angel). They're very nervous
And need considerable jollying. Goose liver,
Cold larks, cranberry tarts and sucking pig,
And now everyone looks as though they only
Wanted to eat each other, which might in the circumstances
Be the best possible thing. Your uncle sent me
To find you. I can tell he's put out; he's as vexed
As a hen's hind feathers in a wind. And for that
Matter so am I. Go back inside
And be jolly like anyone else's children.

NICHOLAS.   Mother,
I'd as soon kiss the bottom of a Barbary ape.
The faces of our friends may be enchantment
To some, but they wrap my spirits in a shroud.—
For the sake of my unborn children, I have to avoid them.
Oh now, be brave, mother. They'll go in the course of nature.

MARGARET. It's unfortunate, considering the wide
Choice of living matter on this globe,
That I should have managed to be a mother. I can't
Imagine what I was thinking of. Your uncle
Has made me shake out the lavender
From one of my first gowns which has hung in the ward-
    robe
Four-and-twenty unencouraging years,
To lend to this Jennet girl, who in my opinion
Should not be here. And I said to her flatly
'The course of events is incredible. Make free
With my jewel box.' Where is she now?

THOMAS.   No doubt
Still making free. Off she has gone,
Away to the melting moody horizons of opal,
Moonstone, bloodstone; now moving in lazy

[65]

Amber, now sheltering in the shade
Of jade from a brief rainfall of diamonds.
Able to think to-morrow has an even
Brighter air, a glitter less moderate,
A quite unparalleled freedom in the fire:
A death, no bounds to it. Where is she now?
She is dressing, I imagine.

MARGARET.   Yes, I suppose so.
I don't like to think of her. And as for you
I should like to think of you as someone I knew
Many years ago, and, alas, wouldn't see again.
That would be charming. I beg you to come,
Humphrey. Give your brother a good example.

HUMPHREY. Mother, I'm unwell.

MARGARET.   Oh, Humphrey!

NICHOLAS.   Mother,
He is officially sick and actually bored.
The two together are as bad as a dropsy.

MARGARET. I must keep my mind as concentrated as possible
On such pleasant things as the summer I spent at Stoke
D'Abernon. Your uncle must do what he will.
I've done what I can.

[*Exit* MARGARET.

NICHOLAS.   Our mother isn't
Pleased.

HUMPHREY. She has never learnt to yawn
And so she hasn't the smallest comprehension
Of those who can.

THOMAS.   Benighted brothers in boredom,
Let us unite ourselves in a toast of ennui.
I give you a yawn: to this evening, especially remembering
Mrs. Cartwright. [*They all yawn.*] To mortal life, women,

[66]

All government, wars, art, science, ambitions,
And the entire fallacy of human emotions!

> [*As they painfully yawn again, enter* JENNET, *bright
> with jewels, and twenty years exquisitely out of fashion.*

JENNET. And wake us in the morning with an ambrosial
Breakfast, amen, amen.
NICHOLAS.   Humphrey, poppin,
Draw back the curtains. I have a sense of daylight.
HUMPHREY. It seems we're facing east.
THOMAS.   You've come too late.
Romulus, Remus and I have just buried the world
Under a heavy snowfall of disinterest.
There's nothing left of life but cranberry tarts,
Goose's liver, sucking pig, cold larks,
And Mrs. Cartwright.
JENNET.   That's riches running mad.
What about the have-not moon? Not a goose, not a pig,
And yet she manages to be the wit
Of heaven, and roused the envious Queen of Sheba
To wash in mercury so that the Sheban fountains
Should splash deliriously in the light of her breast.
But she died, poor Queen, shining less
Than the milk of her thousand shorthorn cows.
THOMAS.   What's this?
Where has the girl I spoke to this evening gone
With her Essential Fact? Surely she knows,
If she is true to herself, the moon is nothing
But a circumambulating aphrodisiac
Divinely subsidized to provoke the world
Into a rising birth-rate—a veneer
Of sheerest Venus on the planks of Time
Which may fool the ocean but which fools not me.

JENNET. So no moon.

THOMAS.   No moon.

NICHOLAS.   Let her have the last quarter.

JENNET.   No;
If he says no moon then of course there can be no moon.
Otherwise we destroy his system of thought
And confuse the quest for truth.

THOMAS.   You see, Nicholas?

JENNET. I've only one small silver night to spend
So show me no luxuries. It will be enough
If you spare me a spider, and when it spins I'll see
The six days of Creation in a web
And a fly caught on the seventh. And if the dew
Should rise in the web, I may well die a Christian.

THOMAS. I must shorten my sail. We're into a strange wind.
This evening you insisted on what you see,
What you touch, what you know. Where did this weather
    blow from?

JENNET. Off the moors of mortality: that might
Be so. Or there's that inland sea, the heart—
But you mustn't hinder me, not now. I come
Of a long-lived family, and I have
Some sixty years to use up almost immediately.
I shall join the sucking pig.

NICHOLAS.   Please take my arm.
I'll guide you there.

HUMPHREY.   He shall do no such thing.
Who's the host here?

THOMAS.   They have impeccable manners
When they reach a certain temperature.

HUMPHREY.   A word
More from you, and you go out of this house.

[68]

THOMAS. Like the heart going out of me, by which it avoids
Having to break.
JENNET.   Be quiet for a moment. I hear
A gay modulating anguish, rather like music.
NICHOLAS. It's the Chaplain, extorting lightness of heart
From the guts of his viol, to the greater glory of God.

Enter HEBBLE TYSON.

TYSON. What I hear from your mother isn't agreeable to me
In the smallest—a draught, quite noticeable.
I'm a victim to air.—I expect members of my family——
THOMAS. Is this courtesy, Mr. Mayor, to turn your back
On a guest?
JENNET.   Why should I be welcome? I am wearing
His days gone by. I rustle with his memories!
I, the little heretic as he thinks,
The all unhallows Eve to his poor Adam;
And nearly stubbing my toes against my grave
In his sister's shoes, the grave he has ordered for me.
Don't ask impossibilities of the gentleman.
TYSON. Humphrey, will you explain yourself?
HUMPHREY.   Uncle,
I came to cool my brow. I was on my way back.
NICHOLAS. Don't keep us talking. I need to plunge again
Into that ice-cap of pleasure in the next room.
I repeat, my arm.
HUMPHREY.   I repeat that I'm the host.
I have the right——
JENNET.   He has the right, Nicholas.
Let me commit no solecism so near
To eternity. Please open the door for us.
We must go in as smoothly as old friends.

            [*Exeunt* JENNET, HUMPHREY, *and* NICHOLAS.

[69]

THOMAS. Well, does your blood run deep enough to run
    Cold, or have you none?
TYSON.   That's enough. Get away.
THOMAS. Are you going to cry-off the burning?
TYSON.   Worthless creatures,
    Both; I call you clutter. The standard soul
    Must mercilessly be maintained. No
    Two ways of life. One God, one point of view.
    A general acquiescence to the mean.
THOMAS. And God knows when you say the mean, you mean
    The mean. You'd be surprised to see the number
    Of cloven hoof-marks in the yellow snow of your soul.
    And so you'll kill her.
    Time would have done it for her too, of course,
    But more cautiously, and with a pretence of charm.
    Am I allowed on bail into your garden?
TYSON. Tiresome catarrh. I haven't any wish to see you,
    Not in the slightest degree: go where you like.
THOMAS. That's nowhere in this world. But still maybe
    I can make myself useful and catch mice for an owl.

                                [*Exit* THOMAS.

Enter TAPPERCOOM.

TAPPERCOOM. The young lunatic slipping off, is he?
    Cheered up and gone? So much the less trouble for us.
    Very jolly evening, Tyson. Are you sober?
TYSON. Yes, yes, yes.
TAPPERCOOM.   You shouldn't say that, you know.
    You're in tears, Tyson. I know tears when I see them,
    My wife has them. You've drunk too deep, my boy.
    Now I'm sober as a judge, perhaps a judge
    A little on circuit, but still sober. Tyson,
    You're in tears, old fellow, two little wandering

Jews of tears getting 'emselves embrangled
In your beard.

TYSON.   I won't stand it, Tappercoom:
I won't have it, I won't have evil things
Looking so distinguished. I'm no longer
Young, and I should be given protection.

TAPPERCOOM.   What
Do you want protecting from now?

TYSON.   We must burn her,
Before she destroys our reason. Damnable glitter.
Tappercoom, we mustn't become bewildered
At our time of life. Too unusual
Not to be corrupt. Must be burnt
Immediately, burnt, burnt, Tappercoom,
Immediately.

TAPPERCOOM. Are you trying to get rid of temptation,
Tyson? A belated visit of the wanton flesh
After all these years? You've got to be dispassionate.
Calm and civilized. I am civilized.
I know, frinstance, that Beauty is not an Absolute.
Beauty is a Condition. As you might say
Hey nonny yes or Hey nonny no.
But the Law's about as absolute an Absolute—
Hello, feeling dicky, Chaplain?

[*The* CHAPLAIN *has entered, crying.*

CHAPLAIN.   It would be
So kind if you didn't notice me. I have
Upset myself. I have no right to exist,
Not in any form, I think.

TAPPERCOOM.   I hope you won't
Think me unsociable if I don't cry myself.
What's the matter? Here's the pair of you
Dripping like newly weighed anchors.

[71]

Let the butterflies come to you, Chaplain,
Or you'll never be pollinated into a Bishop.

CHAPLAIN. No, it's right and it's just I should be cast down.
I've treated her with an abomination
That maketh desolate:—the words, the words
Are from Daniel——

TAPPERCOOM.   Hey, what's this? The young woman again?

CHAPLAIN. My patient instrument. I made my viol
Commit such sins of sound—and I didn't mind:
No, I laughed. I was trying to play a dance.
I'm too unaccomplished to play with any jollity.
I shouldn't venture beyond religious pieces.

TYSON. There's no question of jollity. We've got
To burn her, for our peace of mind.

TAPPERCOOM.   You must wait
Until to-morrow, like a reasonable chap.
And to-morrow, remember, you'll have her property
Instead of your present longing for impropriety.
And her house, now I come to think of it,
Will suit me nicely.
A large mug of small beer for both of you.
Leave it to me.

CHAPLAIN.   No, no, no,
I should become delighted again. I wish
For repentance——

Enter RICHARD.

TAPPERCOOM.   You shall have it. I'll pour it out
Myself. You'll see: it shall bring you to your knees.

CHAPLAIN. I'm too unaccomplished. I haven't the talent,
But I hoped I should see them dancing. And after all
They didn't dance——

[72]

TAPPERCOOM.   They shall, dear saint, they shall.
                    [*Exit* TAPPERCOOM *and the* CHAPLAIN.

RICHARD. I was to tell you, Mr. Tyson——

TYSON.   I'm not
    To be found. I'm fully occupied elsewhere.
    If you wish to find me I shall be in my study.
    You can knock, but I shall give you no reply.
    I wish to be alone with my own convictions.
    Good-night.
                    [*Exit* TYSON. THOMAS *looks through the window.*

                    Enter ALIZON.

THOMAS [*to* RICHARD]. The Great Bear is looking so geo-
    metrical
    One would think that something or other could be proved.
    Are you sad, Richard?

RICHARD.   Certainly.

THOMAS.   I also.
    I've been cast adrift on a raft of melancholy.
    The night-wind passed me, like a sail across
    A blind man's eye. There it is,
    The interminable tumbling of the great grey
    Main of moonlight, washing over
    The little oyster-shell of this month of April:
    Among the raven-quills of the shadows
    And on the white pillows of men asleep:
    The night's a pale pastureland of peace,
    And something condones the world, incorrigibly.
    But what, in fact, *is* this vaporous charm?
    We're softened by a nice conglomeration
    Of the earth's uneven surface, refraction of light,
    Obstruction of light, condensation, distance,
    And that sappy upshot of self-centred vegetablism

                    [73]

The trees of the garden. How is it we come
To see this as a heaven in the eye?
Why should we hawk and spit out ecstasy
As though we were nightingales, and call these quite
Casual degrees and differences
Beauty? What guile recommends the world
And gives our eyes the special sense to be
Deluded, above all animals?—Stone me, Richard!
I've begun to talk like that soulless girl, and she
May at this moment be talking like me! I shall go
Back into the garden, and choke myself with the seven
Sobs I managed to bring with me from the wreck.

RICHARD. To hear her you would think her feet had almost
Left the ground. The evening which began
So blackly, now, as though it were a kettle
Set over her flame, has started to sing. And all
The time I find myself praying under my breath
That something will save her.

THOMAS.   You might do worse.
Tides turn with a similar sort of whisper.

ALIZON. Richard.

RICHARD.   Alizon!

ALIZON.   I've come to be with you.

RICHARD. Not with me. I'm the to-and-fro fellow
To-night. You have to be with Humphrey.

ALIZON.   I think
I have never met Humphrey. I have met him less
And less the more I have seen him.

THOMAS.   You will forgive me.
I was mousing for a small Dutch owl.
If it has said towoo t-wice it has said it
A thousand times.

                    [*He disappears into the garden.*
                    [74]

RICHARD.　　　　　Hey! Thomas—! Ah well.—
　The crickets are singing well with their legs to-night.
ALIZON. It sounds as though the night-air is riding
　On a creaking saddle.
RICHARD.　　　　　You must go back to the others.
ALIZON. Let me stay. I'm not able to love them.
　Have you forgotten what they mean to do
　To-morrow?
RICHARD.　　　　How could I forget? But there are laws
　And if someone fails them——
ALIZON.　　　　　　　　I shall run
　Away from laws if laws can't live in the heart.
　I shall be gone to-morrow.
RICHARD.　　　　　　You make the room
　Suddenly cold. Where will you go?
ALIZON.　　　　　　　　Where
　Will you come to find me?
RICHARD.　　　　　　Look, you've pulled the thread
　In your sleeve. Is it honest for me to believe
　You would be unhappy?
ALIZON.　　　　　When?
RICHARD.　　　　　　　If you marry Humphrey?
ALIZON. Humphrey's a winter in my head.
　But whenever my thoughts are cold and I lay them
　Against Richard's name, they seem to rest
　On the warm ground where summer sits
　As golden as a humblebee.
　So I did very little but think of you
　Until I ran out of the room.
RICHARD.　　　　　　Do you come to me
　Because you can never love the others?
ALIZON.　　　　　　　　Our father
　God moved many lives to show you to me.

[75]

I think that is the way it must have happened.
It was complicated, but very kind.

RICHARD. If I asked you
If you could ever love me, I should know
For certain that I was no longer rational.

ALIZON. I love you quite as much as I love St. Anthony
And rather more than I love St. John Chrysostom.

RICHARD. But putting haloes on one side, as a man
Could you love me, Alizon?

ALIZON. I have become
A woman, Richard, because I love you. I know
I was a child three hours ago. And yet
I love you as deeply as many years could make me,
But less deeply than many years will make me.

RICHARD. I think I may never speak steadily again.
What have I done or said to make it possible
That you should love me?

ALIZON. Everything I loved
Before has come to one meeting place in you
And you have gone out into everything I love.

RICHARD. Happiness seems to be weeping in me, as
I suppose it should, being newly born.

ALIZON. We must never leave each other now, or else
We should perplex the kindness of God.

RICHARD. The kindness
Of God in itself is not a little perplexing.
What do we do?

ALIZON. We cleave to each other, Richard.
That is what is proper for us to do.

RICHARD. But you were promised to Humphrey, Alizon.
And I'm hardly more than a servant here
Tied to my own apron-strings. They'll never
Let us love each other.

[76]

ALIZON.   Then they will have
  To outwit all that ever went to create us.
RICHARD. So they will. I believe it. Let them storm.
  We're lovers in a deep and safe place
  And never lonely any more.—Alizon,
  Shall we make the future, however much it roars,
  Lie down with our happiness? Are you ready
  To forgo custom and escape with me?
ALIZON. Shall we go now, before anyone prevents us?
RICHARD. I'll take you to the old priest who first found me.
  He is as near to being my father
  As putting his hand into a poor-box could make him.
  He'll help us. Oh, Alizon, I so
  Love you. Let yourself quietly out and wait for me
  Somewhere near the gate but in a shadow.
  I must fetch my savings. Are you afraid?
ALIZON.   In some
  Part of me, not all; and while I wait
  I can have a word with the saints Theresa and Christopher:
  They may have some suggestions.
RICHARD.   Yes, do that.
  Now: like a mouse.
                    [*When she has gone he goes to the window.*
                    Only let me spell
  No disillusion for her, safety, peace,
  And a good world, as good as she has made it!
                    [RICHARD *starts to fetch his money.*

                    Enter MARGARET.

MARGARET. Now, Richard: have you found Mr. Tyson?
RICHARD.   Yes;
  He's busy with his convictions.

                    [77]

MARGARET.   He has no business
   To be busy now. How am I to prevent
   This girl, condemned as a heretic, from charming us
   With gentleness, consideration and gaiety?
   It makes orthodoxy seem almost irrelevant.
   But I expect they would tell us the soul can be as lost
   In loving-kindness as in anything else.
   Well, well; we must scramble for grace as best we can.
   Where is Alizon?

RICHARD.   I must—I must——

MARGARET. The poor child has gone away to cry.
   See if you can find her, will you, Richard?

RICHARD. I have to—have to——

MARGARET.   Very well. I will go
   In search of the sad little soul myself.
   Oh dear, I could do with a splendid holiday
   In a complete vacuum.

          [*Exit* MARGARET *one way,* RICHARD, *hastily, another.*

Enter JENNET. *She seems for a moment exhausted, but crosses
   to the window. Enter* NICHOLAS *and* HUMPHREY.

NICHOLAS.   Are you tired of us?

HUMPHREY.   Why on earth
   Can't you stop following her?

NICHOLAS.   Stop following me.

JENNET. I am troubled to find Thomas Mendip.

NICHOLAS.   He's far gone—
   As mad as the nature of man.

HUMPHREY.   As rude and crude
   As an act of God. He'll burn your house.

JENNET.   So he has.—
   Are you kind to mention burning?

HUMPHREY.   I beg your pardon.

[78]

NICHOLAS. Couldn't you to-morrow by some elementary spell
  Reverse the direction of the flames and make them burn
    downwards?
  It would save you unpleasantness and increase at the same
  Time the heat below, which would please
  Equally heaven and hell.
  I feel such a tenderness for you, not only because
  I think you've bewitched my brother, which would be
  A most salutary thing, but because, even more
  Than other women, you carry a sense of that cavernous
  Night folded in night, where Creation sleeps
  And dreams of men. If only we loved each other
  Down the pitshaft of love I could go
  To the motive mysteries under the soul's floor.
  Well drenched in damnation I should be as pure
  As a limewashed wall.
HUMPHREY.   Get out!
JENNET.   He does no harm.—
  Is it possible he still might make for death
  Even on this open-hearted night?
HUMPHREY.   Who might?
JENNET. Thomas Mendip. He's sick of the world, but the world
  Has a right to him.
HUMPHREY.   Damn Thomas Mendip.
NICHOLAS.   Nothing
  Easier.

Enter RICHARD, *upset to see his escape cut off*.

  You're just the fellow, Richard:
  We need some more Canary, say five bottles
  More. And before we go in, we'll drink here, privately,
  To beauty and the sombre sultry waters
  Where beauty haunts.

[79]

RICHARD.   I have to find—to find——

NICHOLAS. Five bottles of Canary. I'll come to the cellars
  And help you bring them. Quick, before our mother
  Calls us back to evaporate into duty.

                    [*Exit* NICHOLAS, *taking* RICHARD *with him.*

HUMPHREY. He's right. You have bewitched me. But not by
    scents
  Of new-mown hell. For all I know you may
  Have had some by-play with the Devil, and your eyes
  May well be violets in a stealthy wood
  Where souls are lost. If so, you will agree
  The fire is fair, as fair goes: you have
  To burn.

JENNET.   It is hard to live last hours
  As the earth deserves. Must you bring closer the time
  When, as night yawns under my feet,
  I shall be cast away in the chasm of dawn?
  I am tired with keeping my thoughts clear of that verge.

HUMPHREY. But need you? These few hours of the night
  Might be lived in a way which wouldn't end
  In fire. It would be insufferable
  If you were burned while you were strange to me.
  I should never sit at ease in my body again.

JENNET. Must we talk of this? All there is
  To be said has been said, and all in a heavy sentence.
  There's nothing to add, except a grave silence.

HUMPHREY. Listen, will you listen? There is more to say.
  I'm able to save you, since all official action
  Can be given official hesitation. I happen
  To be on the Council, and a dozen reasons
  Can be found to postpone the moment of execution:
  Legal reasons, monetary reasons—
  They've confiscated your property, and I can question

Whether your affairs may not be too disordered.
And once postponed, a great congestion of quibbles
Can be let loose over the Council table——

JENNET. Hope can break the heart, Humphrey. Hope
Can be too strong.

HUMPHREY.   But this is true: actual
As my body is. And as for that—now, impartially,
Look what I risk. If in any way you've loosened
The straps which hold in place our fairly workable
Wings of righteousness, and they say you have,
Then my status in both this town and the after-life
Will be gone if either suspect me of having helped you.
I have to be given a considerable reason
For risking that.

JENNET.   I fondly hope I'm beginning
To misconstrue you.

HUMPHREY.   Later on to-night
When they've all gone small into their beauty-sleep
I'll procure the key and come to your cell. Is that
Agreeable?

JENNET.   Is it so to you?
Aren't you building your castles in foul air?

HUMPHREY. Foul? No; it's give and take, the basis
Of all understanding.

JENNET.   You mean you give me a choice:
To sleep with you, or to-morrow to sleep with my fathers.
And if I value the gift of life,
Which, dear heaven, I do, I can scarcely refuse.

HUMPHREY. Isn't that sense?

JENNET.   Admirable sense.
Oh, why, why am I not sensible?
Oddly enough, I hesitate. Can I
So dislike being cornered by a young lecher

That I should rather die? That would be
The maniac pitch of pride. Indeed, it might
Even be sin. Can I believe my ears?
I seem to be considering heaven. And heaven,
From this angle, seems considerable.

HUMPHREY. Now, please, we're not going to confuse the soul
and the body.
This, speaking bodily, is merely an exchange
Of compliments.

JENNET.　　　　　And surely throwing away
My life for the sake of pride would seem to heaven
A bodily blasphemy, a suicide?

HUMPHREY. Even if heaven were interested. Or even
If you cared for heaven. Am I unattractive to you?

JENNET. Except that you have the manners of a sparrowhawk,
With less reason, no, you are not. But even so
I no more run to your arms than I wish to run
To death. I ask myself why. Surely I'm not
Mesmerized by some snake of chastity?

HUMPHREY. This isn't the time——

JENNET.　　　　　　　Don't speak, contemptible boy,
I'll tell you: I am not. We have
To look elsewhere—for instance, into my heart
Where recently I heard begin
A bell of longing which calls no one to church.
But need that, ringing anyway in vain,
Drown the milkmaid singing in my blood
And freeze into the tolling of my knell?
That would be pretty, indeed, but unproductive.
No, it's not that.

HUMPHREY.　　　Jennet, before they come
And interrupt us——

[82]

JENNET.   I am interested
   In my feelings. I seem to wish to have some importance
   In the play of time. If not,
   Then sad was my mother's pain, sad my breath,
   Sad the articulation of my bones,
   Sad, sad my alacritous web of nerves,
   Woefully, woefully sad my wondering brain,
   To be shaped and sharpened into such tendrils
   Of anticipation, to feed the swamp of space.
   What is deep, as love is deep, I'll have
   Deeply. What is good, as love is good,
   I'll have well. Then if time and space
   Have any purpose, I shall belong to it.
   If not, if all is a pretty fiction
   To distract the cherubim and seraphim
   Who so continually do cry, the least
   I can do is to fill the curled shell of the world
   With human deep-sea sound, and hold it to
   The ear of God, until he has appetite
   To taste our salt sorrow on his lips.
   And so you see it might be better to die.
   Though, on the other hand, I admit it might
   Be immensely foolish.—Listen! What
   Can all that thundering from the cellars be?
HUMPHREY. I don't know at all. You're simply playing for
    time.
   Why can't you answer me, before I'm thrown
   By the bucking of my pulse, before Nicholas
   Interrupts us? Will it be all right?
JENNET. Doesn't my position seem pitiable to you?
HUMPHREY. Pitiable, yes. It makes me long for you
   Intolerably. Now, be a saint, and tell me
   I may come to your cell.

JENNET.   I wish I could believe
My freedom was not in the flames. O God, I wish
The ground would open.

                [THOMAS *climbs in through the window.*

THOMAS.   Allow me to open it for you.
Admit I was right. Man's a mistake.
Lug-worms, the lot of us.

HUMPHREY.   Wipe your filthy boots
Before you start trespassing.

THOMAS.   And as for you
I'll knock your apple-blossom back into the roots
Of the Tree of Knowledge where you got it from!

JENNET.   Oh dear,
Is this lug-worms at war? And by what right, will you tell
    me,
Do your long ears come moralizing in
Like Perseus to Andromeda? Pause a moment
And consider.

THOMAS.   Madam, if I were Herod in the middle
Of the massacre of the innocents, I'd pause
Just to consider the confusion of your imagery.

HUMPHREY. If he wants to fight me, let him. Come out in the
    garden.
Whatever happens I shall have one bash at him
Which, next to this other thing, is the most desirable
Act in the world. If he kills me, you and I
The day after to-morrow, can improve
The deadly hours of the grave
By thrashing out the rights and the wrongs of it.
Only remember, I thought you unfairly beautiful
And, to balance your sins, you should be encouraged
For heaven's sake to spend your beauty
In a proper way, on someone who knows its worth.

THOMAS. Sound the trumpets!

JENNET.   Yes, why not? And a roll
Of drums. You, if you remember, failed
Even to give me a choice. You have only said
'Die, woman, and look as though you liked it.'
So you'll agree this can hardly be said to concern you.

THOMAS. All right! You've done your worst. You force me to
     tell you
The disastrous truth. I love you. A misadventure
So intolerable, hell could not do more.
Nothing in the world could touch me
And you have to come and be the damnable
Exception. I was nicely tucked up for the night
Of eternity, and, like a restless dream
Of a fool's paradise, you, with a rainbow where
Your face is and an *ignis fatuus*
Worn like a rose in your girdle, come pursued
By fire, and presto! the bedclothes are on the floor
And I, the tomfool, love you. Don't say again
That this doesn't concern me, or I shall say
That you needn't concern yourself with to-morrow's burn-
     ing.

Enter NICHOLAS.

NICHOLAS. Do you know what that little bastard Richard did?
He locked me in the cellars.

THOMAS.   Don't complicate
The situation.—I love you, perfectly knowing
You're nothing but a word out of the mouth
Of that same planet of almighty blemish
Which I long to leave. But the word is an arrow
Of larksong, shot from the earth's bow, and falling
In a stillborn sunrise.—I shall lie in my grave

[85]

With my hands clapped over my ears, to stop your music
From riddling me as much as the meddling worms.
Still, that's beside the point. We have to settle
This other matter——

NICHOLAS.   Yes, I was telling you.
I went into the cellars to get the wine,
And the door swung after me, and that little son
Of a crossbow turned the key——

THOMAS [to JENNET].   Can we find somewhere
To talk where there isn't quite so much insect life?

NICHOLAS. And there I was, in cobwebs up to my armpits,
Hammering the door and yelling like a slaughter-house,
Until the cook came and let me out. Where is he?

JENNET. What should we talk of? You mean to be hanged.
Am I to understand that your tongue-tied dust
Will slip a ring on the finger of my ashes
And we'll both die happily ever after? Surely
The other suggestion, though more conventional,
Has fewer flaws?

THOMAS.   But you said, like a ray of truth
Itself, that you'd rather burn.

JENNET.   My heart, my mind
Would rather burn. But may not the casting vote
Be with my body? And is the body necessarily
Always ill-advised?

NICHOLAS.   Something has happened
Since I made the descent into those hellish cobwebs.
I'm adrift. What is it?

THOMAS.   Let me speak to her.
You've destroyed my defences, the laborious contrivance
Of hours, the precious pair of you. O Jennet,
Jennet, you should have let me go, before
I confessed a word of this damned word love. I'll not

[86]

Reconcile myself to a dark world
For the sake of five-feet six of wavering light,
For the sake of a woman who goes no higher
Than my bottom lip.

NICHOLAS.   I'll strip and fly my shirt
At the masthead unless someone picks me up.
What has been going on?

THOMAS.   Ask that neighing
Horse-box-kicker there, your matchless brother.

NICHOLAS. Ah, Humphrey darling, have there been
Some official natural instincts?

HUMPHREY.   I've had enough.
The whole thing's become unrecognizable.

JENNET [to THOMAS]. Have I a too uncertain virtue to keep
    you
On the earth?

THOMAS.   I ask nothing, nothing. Stop
Barracking my heart. Save yourself
His way if you must. There will always be
Your moment of hesitation, which I shall chalk
All over the walls of purgatory. Never mind
That, loving you, I've trodden the garden threadbare
Completing a way to save you.

JENNET.   If you saved me
Without wishing to save yourself, you might have saved
Your trouble.

NICHOLAS.   I imagine it's all over with us, Humphrey.
I shall go and lie with my own thoughts
And conceive reciprocity. Come on, you boy of gloom.
The high seas for us.

HUMPHREY.   Oh go and drown yourself
And me with you.

[87]

NICHOLAS. There's no need to drown.
We'll take the tails off mermaids.

Enter MARGARET.

MARGARET. Have any of you
Seen that poor child Alizon? I think
She must be lost.

NICHOLAS. Who isn't? The best
Thing we can do is to make wherever we're lost in
Look as much like home as we can. Now don't
Be worried. She can't be more lost than she was with us.

HUMPHREY. I can't marry her, mother. Could you think
Of something else to do with her?
I'm going to bed.

NICHOLAS. I think Humphrey has been
Improperly making a proper suggestion, mother.
He wishes to be drowned.

MARGARET [*to* THOMAS]. They find it impossible
To concentrate. Have you seen the little
Fair-haired girl?

NICHOLAS. He wishes to be hanged.

MARGARET [*to* JENNET]. Have you hidden the child?

NICHOLAS. She wishes to be burned
Rather than sleep with my brother.

MARGARET. She should be thankful
She can sleep at all. For years I have woken up
Every quarter of an hour. I must sit down.
I'm too tired to know what anyone's saying.

JENNET. I think none of us knows where to look for Alizon.
Or for anything else. But shall we, while we wait
For news of her, as two dispirited women
Ask this man to admit he did no murders?

THOMAS. You think not?

[88]

JENNET.   I know. There was a soldier,
    Discharged and centreless, with a towering pride
    In his sensibility, and an endearing
    Disposition to be a hero, who wanted
    To make an example of himself to all
    Erring mankind, and falling in with a witch-hunt
    His good heart took the opportunity
    Of providing a diversion. O Thomas,
    It was very theatrical of you to choose the gallows.
THOMAS. Mother, we won't listen to this girl.
    She is jealous, because of my intimate relations
    With damnation. But damnation knows
    I love her.
RICHARD [appearing in the doorway]. We have come back.
NICHOLAS. I want to talk to you. Who locked me in the cel-
    lars?
MARGARET [as ALIZON enters]. Alizon, where have you been?
ALIZON.   We had to come back.
MARGARET. Back? From where?
RICHARD.   We came across old Skipps.
ALIZON. We were running away. We wanted to be happy.
NICHOLAS. Skipps?
HUMPHREY.   The body of old Skipps? We'd better
    Find Tappercoom.

                                    [Exit HUMPHREY.
MARGARET.   Alizon, what do you mean,
    Running away?
RICHARD.   He is rather drunk. Shall I bring him
    In? He had been to see his daughter.
JENNET [to THOMAS].   Who
    Will trouble to hang you now?

                                    [She goes up the stairs.

THOMAS [*calling after her*].   He couldn't lie quiet
Among so many bones. He had to come back
To fetch his barrow.

TAPPERCOOM [*entering with* HUMPHREY]. What's all this I'm
told?
I was hoping to hang on my bough for the rest of the evening
Ripe and undisturbed. What is it? Murder
Not such a fabrication after all?

ALIZON. We had to come back, you see, because nobody now
Will be able to burn her.

RICHARD.   Nobody now will be able
To say she turned him into a dog. Come in,
Mr. Skipps.

Enter SKIPPS, *unsteady.*

TAPPERCOOM. It looks uncommonly to me
As though someone has been tampering with the evidence.
Where's Tyson. I'm too amiable to-night
To controvert any course of events whatsoever.

SKIPPS. Your young gentleman says Come in, so I comes in.
Youse only has to say muck off, and I goes, wivout argu-
ment.

TAPPERCOOM. Splendid, of course. Are you the rag-and-bone
merchant of this town, name of Matthew Skipps?

SKIPPS. Who give me that name? My granfathers and gran-
mothers and all in authorority undrim. Baptized I blaming
was, and I says to youse, baptized I am, and I says to youse,
baptized I will be, wiv holy weeping and washing of teeth.
And immersion upon us miserable offenders. Miserable offenders all—no offence meant. And if any of youse is not a
miserable offender, as he's told to be by almighty and mer-
cerable God, then I says to him Hands off my daughter,
you bloody-minded heathen.

[90]

TAPPERCOOM. All right, all right——

SKIPPS. And I'm not quarrelling, mind; I'm not quarrelling. Peace on earth and good tall women. And give us our trespassers as trespassers will be prosecuted for us. I'm not perfect, mind. But I'm as good a miserable offender as any man here present, ladies excepted.

THOMAS. Here now, Matt, aren't you forgetting yourself? You're dead: you've been dead for hours.

SKIPPS. Dead, am I? I has the respect to ask you to give me coabberation of that. I says mucking liar to nobody. But I seen my daughter three hours back, and she'd have said fair and to my face Dad, you're dead. She don't stand for no nonsense.

NICHOLAS. The whole town knows it, Skipps, old man. You've been dead since this morning.

SKIPPS. Dead. Well, you take my breaf away. Do I begin to stink, then?

HUMPHREY. You do.

SKIPPS. Fair enough. That's coabberation. I'm among the blessed saints.

TAPPERCOOM. He floats in the heaven of the grape. Someone take him home to his hovel.

SKIPPS [*roaring*]. Alleluia! Alleluia! Alleluia!

TAPPERCOOM. Now, stop that, Skipps. Keep your hosannas for the cold light of morning or we shall lock you up.

SKIPPS. Alleluia!

TAPPERCOOM. He'll wake your guests and spoil their pleasure. They're all sitting half sunk in a reef of collars. Even the dear good Chaplain has taken so many glassesful of repentance he's almost unconscious of the existence of sin.

SKIPPS. Glory, amen! Glory, glory, amen, amen!

MARGARET. Richard will take this old man home. Richard——

Where is Richard? Where is Alizon?
Have they gone again?

NICHOLAS. Yes; Humphrey's future wife,
Blown clean away.

MARGARET. Yes; that's all very well;
But she mustn't think she can let herself be blown
Away whenever she likes.

THOMAS. What better time
Than when she likes?

SKIPPS. As it was in the beginning,
Ever and ever, amen, al-leluia!

MARGARET. Take the old man to his home. Now that you've
made him
Think he's dead we shall never have any peace.

HUMPHREY. Nor shall we when he's gone.

NICHOLAS. Spread your wings, Matthew; we're going to teach
you to fly.

SKIPPS. I has the respect to ask to sit down. Youse blessed saints
don't realize: it takes it out of you, this life everlasting.
Alleluia!

NICHOLAS. Come on.
Your second wind can blow where no one listens.

[*Exeunt* HUMPHREY, NICHOLAS, *and* SKIPPS.

TAPPERCOOM. That's more pleasant.
What was the thread, now, which the rascal broke?
Do I have to collect my thoughts any further?

MARGARET. Yes:
Or I must. That poor child Alizon
Is too young to go throwing herself under the wheels
Of happiness. She should have wrapped up warmly first.
Hebble must know, in any case. I must tell him,
Though he's locked himself in, and only blows his nose
When I knock.

TAPPERCOOM.   Yes, get him on to a horse;
   It will do him good.
MARGARET.   Hebble on a horse is a man
   Delivered neck and crop to the will of God.
   But he'll have to do it.

                                    [*Exit* MARGARET.
TAPPERCOOM.   Ah yes, he'll have to do it.
   He's a dear little man.—What's to be the end of you?
   I take it the male prisoner is sufficiently
   Deflated not to plague us with his person
   Any longer?
THOMAS.   Deflated? I'm overblown
   With the knowledge of my villainy.
TAPPERCOOM.   Your guilt, my boy,
   Is a confounded bore.
THOMAS.   Then let it bore me to extinction.
                [JENNET *returns, wearing her own dress.*
TAPPERCOOM. The woman prisoner may notice, without
   My mentioning it, that there's a certain mildness
   In the night, a kind of somnolent inattention.
   If she wishes to return to her cell, no one
   Can object. On the other hand—How very empty
   The streets must be just now.—You will forgive
   A yawn in an overworked and elderly man.—
   The moon is full, of course. To leave the town
   Unobserved, one would have to use caution. As for me
   I shall go and be a burden to my bed.
   Good night.
JENNET.   Good night.
THOMAS.   Good night.
                                 [*Exit* TAPPERCOOM.
THOMAS.   So much for me.

                    [93]

JENNET.   Thomas, only another
Fifty years or so and then I promise
To let you go.

THOMAS.   Do you see those roofs and spires?
There sleep hypocrisy, porcous pomposity, greed,
Lust, vulgarity, cruelty, trickery, sham
And all possible nitwittery—are you suggesting fifty
Years of that?

JENNET.   I was only suggesting fifty
Years of me.

THOMAS.   Girl, you haven't changed the world.
Glimmer as you will, the world's not changed.
I love you, but the world's not changed. Perhaps
I could draw you up over my eyes for a time
But the world sickens me still.

JENNET.   And do you think
Your gesture of death is going to change it? Except
For me.

THOMAS.   Oh, the unholy mantrap of love!

JENNET. I have put on my own gown again,
But otherwise everything that is familiar,
My house, my poodle, peacock, and possessions,
I have to leave. The world is looking frozen
And forbidding under the moon; but I must be
Out of this town before daylight comes, and somewhere,
Who knows where, begin again.

THOMAS.   Brilliant!
So you fall back on the darkness to defeat me.
You gamble on the possibility
That I was well-brought-up. And, of course, you're right.
I have to see you home, though neither of us
Knows where on earth it is.

[94]

JENNET.   Thomas, can you mean to let
   The world go on?
THOMAS.   I know my limitations.
   When the landscape goes to seed, the wind is obsessed
   By to-morrow.
JENNET.   I shall have to hurry.
   That was the pickaxe voice of a cock, beginning
   To break up the night. Am I an inconvenience
   To you?
THOMAS.   As inevitably as original sin.
   And I shall be loath to forgo one day of you,
   Even for the sake of my ultimate friendly death.
JENNET. I am friendly too.
THOMAS.   Then let me wish us both
   Good morning.—And God have mercy on our souls.

THE CURTAIN FALLS

[95]